Terrorism, Freedom, and Security

The BCSIA Studies in International Security book series is edited at the Belfer Center for Science and International Affairs at Harvard University's John F. Kennedy School of Government and published by The MIT Press. The series publishes books on contemporary issues in international security policy, as well as their conceptual and historical foundations. Topics of particular interest to the series include the spread of weapons of mass destruction, internal conflict, the international effects of democracy and democratization, and U.S. defense policy.

A complete list of BCSIA Studies in International Security appears at the back of this volume.

Terrorism, Freedom, and Security

Winning without War

Philip B. Heymann

The MIT Press
Cambridge, Massachusetts
London, England

© 2003 Philip B. Heymann

Printed and bound in the United States of America.

Library of Congress Cataloging-in-Publication Data

Heymann, Philip B.
Terrorism, freedom, and security : winning without war /
Philip B. Heymann.
p.   cm.—(BCSIA studies in international security)
Includes bibliographical references and index.
ISBN 0-262-08327-2 (hc : alk. paper)
1. Terrorism—United States—Prevention. 2. Terrorism—
Government policy—United States. I. Title. II. Series.

HV6432.H494   2003
363.3'2'0973—dc21   2003051126

10   9   8   7   6   5   4   3   2   1

As always, to my manager, Ann.
Also, to our latest generation—Paul, Becca, Ben, and Jeremy.
May they share the 21st century with pride in their nation,
secure in their freedoms.

Contents

Acknowledgments

Jointly teaching a Harvard Law School course in "Terrorism after September 11, 2001" with two wonderful colleagues, Dean Louise Richardson and Dr. Ariel Merari, inspired me to write this book. Kate Farrington, with patience, industry, and friendship, produced the manuscript. Two law school students, Michael Kleinman and Matthew Hillery, helped to research, criticize, and edit it, managing the work of a number of other dedicated student researchers. Sean Lynn-Jones of the Kennedy School of Government guided it through the process to publication. All have my sincere appreciation.

Preface

"Perhaps it is a universal truth that the loss of liberty at home is to be charged to provisions against danger, real or pretended, from abroad." (Letter of James Madison to Thomas Jefferson, May 13, 1798)

"To lose our country by a scrupulous adherence to written law would be to lose the law itself, with life, liberty, property and all those who are enjoying them with us; thus absurdly sacrificing the end to the means." (Letter from Thomas Jefferson to John B. Colvin, September 20, 1810)

Much has changed since my book *Terrorism and America* was first published in 1998. A war in Iraq and a war in Afghanistan, with both the resentment and the loss of havens they created for terrorism, have followed the frightening attacks of September 11, 2001, changing the landscape for addressing terrorism. This book is about those changes—particularly the radical change brought about by the Al Qaeda attack—and what we can and should do about new, heightened dangers. But its message is also that some things have not changed: the necessity of assessing the effectiveness of the steps we take; the need to recognize that the same step that helps to reduce terrorism in one way can, in another way, increase it; and, foremost, the importance of remaining acutely aware of the non-dollar costs of what we do. We must recognize costs as well as benefits, looking at the future as well as the present.

Borrowing from Oscar Wilde, Churchill said that in war nothing succeeds like excess. In war we need a surge of costly activities—ignoring for a short time (less than four years of World War II) not only vast displacement of the economy but also many of the democratic liberties we are fighting to maintain. Analogously, in times of urgent but temporary private danger, the criminal law around the world allows a citizen to kill or take another's property. In times of urgent but temporary national danger, we draft young men and send them to where they may be killed. In war, we have to temporarily ignore liberties and even carelessly excessive costs.

However, terrorism is not a threat that is temporary. We cannot count on ending a phenomenon that can be brought about by any small group in a world of seven billion people. And we cannot allow such small and hostile groups to impose on us for decades the costs we would be prepared to bear for a few years to protect ourselves against the vast powers of an advanced foreign state.

Nor is terrorism a form of attack that is met effectively by a sudden but unsustainable surge of actions whose costs often exceed their benefits. No sensible person would complain of savings that could have been made in World War II by more careful calculation of effective and efficient means or tactics. There was no time for that. But terrorism is different. Attorney General John Ashcroft made just such a calculation in cutting the FBI's budget request for fighting terrorism on September 10, 2001; and President George W. Bush rejected Congressional spending levels for the same purposes in 2002. And no sensible person would fail to consider the dangers of a power, claimed by the president, to detain American citizens in secret locations and without trial for the duration of terrorist attacks from abroad on the United States.

Three requirements remain constant about our response to new, far greater threats of terrorism after September 11, despite loose analogies of a "war on terror" to a war with Nazi Germany and Imperial Japan. First, we have to think hard about what we know, and can learn, about what may be effective. Second, we have to recognize that in this effort, unlike in real war, what helps in one way is likely to be damaging in another. The reason for this is simple. Terrorism is almost always the tactic of those who feel powerless or purposely disempowered. Actions that restrain their dangerous activities are likely to increase their resentment at powerlessness or repression. Assassinating a terrorist leader may weaken management but, by creating a martyr, help recruitment. Third, we cannot ignore the costs to democracy of steps taken in a prolonged effort to deal with a form of attack that will continue to be available to small numbers of angry people for decades.

That simple message provides the organization of this book. Chapters 1 and 2 address what happened, what changed, and the recklessness of addressing a difficult array of important issues by reciting the word "war" or simply turning them over to the people who fight real wars. Chapters 3 and 4 describe what can and cannot reduce the threat of terrorism and explore how steps that reduce the threat can also increase it. Certainly the experience of Israel should remind us of that possibility. These chapters assess the net benefits of steps we can take.

The non-dollar costs in democratic liberties and risks to future world leadership are the subject of Chapters 5 and 6. Our best guess at these costs has to be "subtracted" from our best guess as to the net gains in reduced terrorism. Otherwise, small hostile groups—perhaps fewer than 100 persons—can reshape the institutions and understandings that have served America so well for two centuries.

The final chapters focus on how we can organize the government to gather the information we will need without becoming an "intelligence state."

Part I

Real and Metaphorical "War"

Chapter 1

Terrorism after September 11

In 1998, I wrote a book explaining terrorism as we knew it then. In a new preface for a reprinting in 2000, I emphasized the already growing fears that nuclear and biological weapons of mass destruction would be used by terrorists. Understanding the threat to America of terrorism after September 11, 2001 requires understanding what the situation was before that date and what changed with that attack and with ensuing wars in Afghanistan and Iraq.

Terrorism as We Knew It before September 11

Perhaps the most important point for any student of terrorism to recognize before September 11 was that, for reasons not totally understood, a little bit of terrorism goes a long way. Even small-scale terrorism possesses an almost magical ability to produce fear, anxiety, anger, and a demand for vigorous action in a sizeable portion of a country's population. A handful of terrorists led Canadian Prime Minister Pierre Trudeau to declare a state of emergency in Quebec province.[1] Belgium responded powerfully to a similar concern flowing from an equally small group.[2] The Red Army Faction, which preoccupied Germany for more than two decades, rarely had more than a few active members.[3] Even the Provisional IRA at its most active in Northern Ireland involved only hundreds, not thousands, of armed opponents of the British government.[4]

These small groups were able to reshape the domestic and foreign agendas of great governments even though the level of harm they threatened was very low and their means, with few exceptions, conventional. For more than 100 years, starting in the late nineteenth century, terrorists restricted themselves to assassinations, hostage-taking (which now includes hijacking of planes), and setting off relatively conventional bombs. The lesson for governments was to do what was necessary to protect citizens against a danger that was far less threatening than war or depression while guarding democratic liberties against the anger and fear that terrorism produced.

Before September 11, the United States was dealing with a terrorist problem that, with what then seemed to be two remarkable exceptions—the bombing of the World Trade Center in 1993, and the bombing in 1995 of the Alfred P. Murrah Federal Building in Oklahoma City—posed minimal risks at home. The harm to U.S. citizens abroad from much more troublesome international terrorism was also very small. The danger to our embassies manifested by the attacks in Kenya and Tanzania in 1998 was serious but did not create intense fear and anxiety at home, although we were already seeing the hands of Osama bin Laden and his Al Qaeda organization behind them. The result, as FBI and CIA testimony before the Congressional Intelligence Committees after September 11 has confirmed, was that there was relatively little concern about prevention of attacks in the United States.

How dangerous a situation is depends not only on how bad it is currently—and we were enjoying a prolonged period of safety at home—but also on how likely the situation is to get worse. We saw no particular reason to fear a radical increase in terrorism. Terrorism could threaten us in any one of the following four ways, none of which seemed likely: (1) we could anticipate a higher probability of the type of relatively small attacks against American interests, largely abroad, that we experienced in the 1980s; but these had gone down in the 1990s.

(2) More seriously, we could anticipate a sustained campaign of bombings such as those France and Britain had experienced in the 1980s and 1990s. Nothing promised that. (3) We had seen a handful of spectacular terrorist events involving conventional explosives used as powerful car or truck bombs. True, there was the World Trade Center bombing of 1993, and the bombing of the Murrah Building in Oklahoma City, but most attacks were overseas. There were the attacks on the American embassies in Africa and on the Khobar Towers barracks in Saudi Arabia, two large attacks in Lebanon, and more, but these seemed to show that it was easier, and thus more tempting, for terrorists to attack American forces and diplomats abroad than ordinary citizens at home. (4) Finally, we were beginning to worry about weapons of mass destruction, particularly nuclear and biological devices, but nothing like that had been seen with the sole exception of the limited Aum Shinrikyo sarin gas attacks in Japan.[5]

Our attention was focused on how to deal with hostage takers and how to retaliate after a terrorist event. Thus there was little attention paid to prevention, particularly at home. As a result, the September 11 terrorists were hardly challenged in their use of easily hijacked airliners as humanly guided missiles to attack targets that were both symbolic and important.

Prior to September 11, it was possible to describe, with some precision, what options the United States had in dealing with the two most familiar forms of attack by terrorists: hostage taking or deadly attacks against people and property. Terrorists were likely to hijack or take hostages in other forms because of the immense publicity associated with the prolonged detention of, and prolonged danger to, U.S. citizens. Since the object of terrorism is, overwhelmingly, to use the magically exaggerated fear, anger, and anxiety that even a few terrorists can create as a megaphone to speak to audiences that would not otherwise hear or listen,[6] hostage taking had great publicity advantages. The options for a state whose hostages were taken were either to try to rescue them with a sudden military-like assault, or to make concessions to the demands of the terrorists. Otherwise there was nothing to do but stall.

If instead the terrorists had killed a state's citizens or destroyed its property, the remedies took the form of retaliation designed, much like criminal punishment, not only to deter future attacks but also to reassure the public of the targeted nation that they were not helpless and that their leaders were not indifferent. If the United States could satisfy itself and its allies that the attacks were state-sponsored, it could rely on the international law of self-defense to justify a short retaliatory military response, as we did in Libya, Iraq, Sudan, and Afghanistan; or it could attempt to establish diplomatic, economic, or travel sanctions, which required the cooperation of at least the major economies, or secure a UN Security Council resolution like the one that imposed sanctions on Libya after the bombing of Pan Am Flight 103.

If we could not attribute the attack to a state, we could attempt to respond against the individual terrorists or their organization. If the terrorists had fled to another state, that would require extradition as well as assistance in gathering evidence abroad. These forms of cooperation were often not forthcoming from states that either sympathized with the terrorists or feared that the terrorists, who had not bothered them before, would retaliate against them for extraditing someone belonging to one of their organizations. Without the formalities of extradition, a sanctuary state could agree to our arresting someone there. Pakistan did that in the case of Ramsi Yousef, the leader of the 1993 bombing of the World Trade Center. As an alternative, the United States could try to capture the terrorists abroad without the cooperation of a foreign government, a step forbidden by international law and the law of the state where the terrorists were seeking sanctuary. Israel had done this in the case of Adolf Eichmann; we, in the case of the Mexican killers of American DEA agent Enrique Camarena-Salazar.[7]

What Changed on September 11, 2001

What changed on September 11, 2001? First, the ruthlessness and devastation of the attacks convinced us that terrorists targeting the United States would in fact use weapons of mass destruction, including nuclear and biological weapons, if they could obtain and deliver them. Iraq had seemed a likely source. Second, the careful planning and professional execution with which the September 11 attacks were carried out; the attribution of the attacks to an organization, Al Qaeda, which may have trained more than 10,000 would-be terrorists; and the location of that large organization within a context of radical Islamism that may motivate millions—these together created a form and scale of threat totally different from that posed by the handful of largely untrained terrorist operatives we had seen in the past. Moreover, what we could conclude from the September 11 attacks alone cast new light on—had to be reconsidered in the light of—the successful embassy bombings and the near success of the 1993 attack on the World Trade Center.

The first implication of these changes was that our estimation of the size of the danger we faced from terrorism, whether measured by the people attacking us or by the weapons they might use, was suddenly increased by several orders of magnitude. The implication of this was that we had to start taking the problems of prevention and consequence-management vastly more seriously—more seriously, indeed, than the problems of hostage-taking and retaliation that had been our focus before.

Broadly, prevention had two or three aspects: keeping the terrorist events from happening; dealing with the consequences effectively if they did happen; and restoring national confidence thereafter. The first, which took on far greater urgency after September 11, also suddenly looked more difficult because we were dealing with suicide bombers, whose effectiveness was being demonstrated daily in Israel. They had a distinct tactical advantage. Among the half-dozen or so challenges for terrorists designing a successful attack, one had been eliminated: the necessity of planning for the terrorists' escape.

Our ideas about how order was to be imposed on the world's politics also changed on September 11. Until the end of the twentieth century, the relevant set of legal arrangements—the morally binding and somewhat enforceable rules—could be described as a complex network of powers and responsibilities. Most law dealing with terrorism was left to the decision of specific states. Some was created by mutual agreement among sovereign states through bilateral treaties (such as the extradition agreements between the United States and scores of nations) or by multilateral conventions (such as the United Nations Charter or the airplane sabotage convention). Subject to veto, the Security Council could direct states to take (or refrain from) actions where necessary to secure or maintain peace. For example, it imposed sanctions on Libya as a result of the attack on Pan Am Flight 103 over Lockerbie.

What states could do in the name of fighting terrorism was limited in another way. States could and did agree to protect certain fundamental human rights of their own citizens or citizens of other states. By the start of the twenty-first century, many nations, but not including the United States, had even agreed to accept and cooperate with the jurisdiction of an International Criminal Court that could, at the behest of its first prosecutor, Luis Moreno Ocampo, enforce a few of the most basic of these rights against officials and other individuals throughout the world. On less basic matters, an individual state could hold another state responsible for the fair treatment of its citizens when residing as aliens abroad. Aside from these relatively minor restrictions, each state was responsible for the peaceful and useful relations among people within its borders.

While a state could enforce its own laws against terrorism by citizens or aliens—individuals or organizations—within its territory, subject only to its obligations by treaty or tradition to respect human rights and also to protect, in specified ways, citizens of other countries, it could not regulate or prohibit actions abroad except those by its own citizens or those actions directed at consequences within the state or threatening the nation itself. (One further but narrow power allowed every state to punish violations of a very few "universal" norms respecting behavior no state could handle alone or tolerate being left unhandled.) Theoretically State X might order its citizens in State Y to do something State Y prohibited for anyone within its borders, but that possible conflict arose *very* rarely if ever.

Thus, whether the actions involved states, groups, or individuals, it was decently clear who had the power to regulate their relationships. There were no sizeable gaps—no significant areas of dispute about whose or what law controlled whether a governmental or non-governmental organization or an individual was free to take action A. And the understanding about who could enforce the rules setting any applicable limits for permissible actions was almost equally clear. A state could take military action against another state only in self-defense and pending Security Council response. Other forms of sanction—economic or diplomatic—were only restricted by specific agreements (such as trade agreements). No state could enforce its laws by sending its police into any other state without consent of the host country.

September 11 revealed a gap in this web of legal regimes for states, groups, and individuals that had been intended to deal comprehensively with war, crime, and the rights of non-citizens. Al Qaeda was a sizeable non-governmental organization, operating from a number of states against the people and government of the United States, thereby creating a threat to the lives, physical security, and economic welfare of U.S. citizens and residents. It posed an ongoing danger of attack and harm much larger than that of any purely criminal group, yet it generally operated without ongoing support of a hostile state (thus not making applicable even an extended notion of the power of self-defense against a hostile state). Its activities could be prohibited as crimes against the United States under the rules allowing each state to protect itself against crimes targeting that state. But it planned, trained, and frequently operated beyond the area where we can *enforce* our laws by sending in police, leaving us to rely on schemes of international cooperation never designed to bear the strain of a systematic set of attacks on our country.

Its first attack relied on visitors from other countries, a category whose relatively free entry into and life within the United States had hitherto been welcomed. Welcoming alien visitors had not posed any comparable danger in peacetime, although "enemy aliens" had traditionally experienced severe controls in time of war between the United States and the state of their citizenships.

In short, even extending the rights of nations to defend themselves to include attacks on states knowingly harboring a terrorist group would not make the familiar laws of war available to the United States when Al Qaeda operated in secret from friendly states. And even extending the network of law enforcement cooperation would not create a system, in every state from which Al Qaeda might operate, sufficiently motivated and efficient to prevent attacks on us. A dangerous gap remained.

The President responded by expanding the notion of international war, previously limited almost exclusively to conflict among states, to reach foreign non-state groups that wanted to harm the United States—and invoking, with the expanded use of "war," the extraordinary powers of a wartime executive at home and some of the powers associated in the past with controlling "enemy aliens" in wartime. Because our non-state enemies in this "war" did not comply with the obligations that states had accepted in the Geneva Conventions, we noted and exploited the absence of international law protection against their being detained indefinitely, tried by the military, and coercively interrogated.

Even as to states the rules changed. Eighteen months after the attack, the Director of Policy Planning at the Department of State, Richard Haass,[8] had developed a notion of "weak sovereignty," something less than the traditional rights of sovereignty, which was to be the fate of nations that either support terrorist movements; or possess weapons of mass destruction in violation of international law; or engage in repeated breaches of human rights. Any of these activities could justify a military intervention. With that, traditional notions of sovereign rights to be free of foreign interventions, ranging from police operations to war, had joined domestic traditions as the subjects of proposed radical transformation.

Already, in the name of a "war" of a new kind, the president had asserted new claims of executive powers to act without normal legislation or judicial review; to maintain wartime secrecy in place of public accountability; and to detain even citizens without allegations of crime or judicial determination of dangerousness. Now the nation claimed a right to operate militarily in countries with which we are at peace to capture or kill our attackers. For such illegal combatants in a "war" (albeit of an unprecedented, non-state form) against the United States and for the states where they resided, there was a new absence of protection from U.S. actions. The United States could make its own rules—which generally showed restraint—and the commander in chief alone could speak for the United States in making them.

What We Still Did Not Know

If the world looked startlingly different to the public, it was not because we had much specific information about the nature of the threat. Assessing the more precise nature of a terrorist threat requires understanding the motivation of the terrorists, their organizational structure, and their capabilities, including their access to needed resources. As to each of these, the American public and, to a large extent, our government was quite ignorant. We could not answer certain crucial questions, even after our overthrow of the Taliban and our pursuit of members of Al Qaeda in Afghanistan and in the rest of the world.

The motivation of Al Qaeda might have been to drive the United States out of Saudi Arabia and bring us to end our support of Israel; alternatively, it might have been to harvest and redirect the frustrations, resentments, and sense of lost respect of some significant proportion of over a billion Muslims.[9] The first would suggest targets in the future that would have the maximum impact on American people. The second would lead Al Qaeda to look for targets that were most inspiring in the symbolism of the Muslim world.

As to structure, Al Qaeda could be a hierarchical organization whose capacities would be greatly diminished if it were deprived of a home base from which its leadership could operate. But, alternatively, it might be more like a franchising operation or a foundation, reviewing plans and then funding much smaller groups of independent operators and helping them make the necessary contacts for carrying out their plans. Somewhere in between, it could be a terrorist training and indoctrination facility for the thousands who visited its bases in Afghanistan, many of whom might then return with plans needing more specific assistance.

The minimal conditions for operating even something as small in scale as a terrorist foundation would be an ability to raise money, a reliable system for inviting and vetting applicants, a pool of dedicated people who may want to submit plans, and a group of trusted individuals who could provide the missing expertise or resources needed for execution of an applicant's plan. The most significant difference from a hierarchical organization is the absence of any need for a substantial home base or headquarters. Indeed, the organization could be even less structured: largely a religious/social movement based on hostility to the United States because of conditions that are blamed on U.S. policy.

Finally, whatever the structure and motivation, the capabilities of the terrorists depend upon skills, weapons, helpers abroad, and support available within the United States, as well as what money the organization has available to it. The professionalism of the attacks on September 11 suggests deliberation, careful planning, and disciplined execution but tells us little else about the capacity of the organization. We were wholly unprepared for an event that, in retrospect, involved stunningly little in the way of sophisticated technology.

We can take truly effective steps of prevention only if we know something about motivation, organizational structure, and capabilities. Only if we know these matters can we also assess how much in the way of dollars and historic liberties we must be prepared to pay for more adequate prevention.

The Response of the Bush Administration

Faced with these risks and these uncertainties, the Bush administration defined the dangers we faced as "war," demanding and justifying a radical shifting of our domestic and international priorities. It waged a traditional "war" against the Taliban in Afghanistan, denying Al Qaeda their former safe haven, and a far less successful pursuit of the leaders of Al Qaeda.[10] It explained a war against Iraq as needed to deal with the danger that Saddam Hussein would make weapons of mass destruction available to Al Qaeda or similar others. At home, it acted as if we were confronted with the risks to our independence, safety, and economy that existed during World War II. It challenged boldly, if not brashly, traditional assumptions about our democratic freedoms and the role of judicial review in guaranteeing them. And it excluded the Congress as far as possible from responsibility for determining what steps could and should be taken and even from oversight of the conduct of the "war." Finally, our allies were "either with us or against us," as we decided largely by ourselves what had to be done.[11]

The administration's focus was sharply on prevention of future attacks and the use of "offense" against terrorist groups to accomplish this and reduce fear. Increasing safety was a sensible dominant aim, although as a nation we have additional concerns as well. We have to maintain our foreign alliances, formal and informal. That requires not only mutual benefit but also maintaining a persuasive moral and legal justification behind our military, diplomatic, and economic actions abroad. We have to maintain trust in—and avoid fear of—our government for all significant parts of the population. That requires both effectiveness and fairness in our responses. We want to punish wrongdoers simply because that's right, and we would like to build as broad as possible a military, legal, and moral commitment to oppose all forms of terrorism—even those that do not threaten us. But no other goal is quite comparable in importance to creating safety and ending fear.

Recognizing the concern about fairness and maintaining trust in our government among all significant sections of the population, the administration tried to avoid a war on the Muslim religion, successfully seeking support against Al Qaeda from Muslim countries. At home, when it felt that particular groups had to be subjected to exceptional steps of investigation, it announced a focus on aliens (frequently not distinguishing between resident aliens and visitors) while in practice giving particular attention to aliens from Arab or Muslim countries (no other terrorist group threatening the United States had made use of suicide bombers).[12] The administration showed a willingness to spend very large amounts of money and to extensively reorganize the federal government in an effort to prevent future terrorist attacks and, more sparingly, to reduce the harmful consequences of those that would occur.

In one sense, these were the actions of an administration that, even prior to September 11, was skeptical of Congress and the courts, unconcerned with traditional domestic priorities, and doubtful of the need for international cooperation. But these responses also reflect the central mystery of even the most conventional form of terrorism: a capacity to generate massive fear and anxiety. Public fears and anger are immediate and powerful; threats to civil liberties or divisions within the society or among allies are more remote and far less urgent or demanding. Moreover, in the background lies the time bomb of political responsibility for not having stopped the next terrorist attack, whether it is a small conventional bomb, a campaign of conventional bombings, a "spectacular," or an effort to use chemical, biological, or nuclear weapons. We may not know much about the real risks that face us, but political actors can assess the political costs to be borne by anyone who has opposed even the most extravagant of preventive steps, if and when the next terrorist event takes place.

The Wisdom of War in Afghanistan

Whatever one's views on the wisdom of trying to reduce the dangers of terrorism by attacking Iraq in 2003, the initial commitment to war in Afghanistan was plainly wise. Al Qaeda was able to recruit, train, plan, and marshal resources to attack far more easily because the government of Afghanistan tolerated and supported these activities. Much of the world was prepared to accept our expanded definition of national self-defense—the standard required by Article 51 of the UN Charter—when we declared that harboring those activities was a hostile threat to U.S. security. We have dealt with that state support by a military campaign that should also be a warning to other states. Such open help will not be available, risk free, in the future to groups threatening violence against U.S. citizens and interests at home or abroad.

War in Afghanistan had other benefits. Much of the motivation for the attacks on September 11 may have been to turn the passive resentment of felt victimization into heroic hopes in much of Islam by showing the vulnerability of the United States to Islamist terrorists and proving its inability to retaliate effectively. This would increase enthusiasm for violent action in any pool of people deeply hostile to the United States. Our successful war in Afghanistan has helped deny these dangerous rewards to terrorists.

Indeed, the war in Afghanistan promised to show our enemies that we had learned how to fight and win wars without bearing grave losses of our own soldiers' lives; in some unstable nations even a relatively weak armed opposition becomes powerful, compared to the government it resists, when intelligently supported by our air power and Special Forces. Finally, to whatever extent we have been able to capture or kill individuals planning to continue the attacks of September 11 or to deny them the resources they need, we have also been addressing the danger even if in fact our efforts reach only a fraction of our potential enemies and of their resources.

Other factors favored treating the conflict with the Taliban as a war. The conflict depended in far larger measure on the activities of the U.S. military than on intelligence agencies, the State Department, or the Justice Department. The number of armed and dangerous individuals we faced was beyond the operational capacity and beyond the physical reach of our judicial system. Useful or even necessary measures involving a significant amount of collateral damage depended for their legality on this being a war. The conflict, insofar as it was against the Taliban regime of Afghanistan, would have a limited duration during which it would require extraordinary mobilization of our resources and prompt, centralized decision-making. The conflict was far more analogous to what we had called "wars" in the Middle East and South Asia than what we had labeled "terrorism" in those areas.

More Questionable Choices

The administration announced a goal of destroying any form of terrorism that could threaten us and, perhaps, terrorism more broadly, almost regardless of the cost.[13] That goal seemed so obviously a pre-condition for civilization—nothing justified attacking innocent civilians for political purposes—that the administration demanded unqualified support from other countries as a measure of their friendship and their recognition of the harm that had been done to us. We did not address the issue with our friends as a problem of foreign relations that could be confronted in any number of ways, and as to which good friends could differ. You were with us or against us.

⇒ The administration needed support at home, too. It relied on public fears and the resulting demands for vigorous, unified leadership to corral the Congress. Its insistence on the importance of secrecy, and therefore the impropriety of oversight, helped. Its political posture was always aggressive, for the administration trusted that the American people would not demand greater deference to allies or to domestic civil liberties.

Finally, for structures and resources needed to crush terrorism, the administration relied primarily on the Department of Defense and secondarily on a new Department of Homeland Security. Improved intelligence was important, but it was felt that the FBI and the CIA could work that out with sufficient pressure from the president and the Congress. The role of the State Department was largely to maintain support abroad for our military efforts.

In the chapters that follow, I shall argue that however well that strategy might work in the short term, it has great weaknesses as a long-term strategy. War on terrorism is the wrong theme. Reliance on the military is the wrong set of priority activities. We need the willing cooperation of allies throughout the world, and this will require taking into account views of terrorist activity as something other than pure evil. Continued domestic support will depend upon confidence that the administration is not proposing, as "temporary" losses of democratic liberties, changes that could last for generations. Most important, the organizational structure that is most needed is a greatly improved intelligence apparatus that will still be accountable to the American people. Expenditures on the departments of Defense and Homeland Security might be worthwhile, but they are, ultimately, of secondary importance.

Many administration decisions looked fine in the short run. There are, however, special requirements for a government project that is intended to last over a sustained period of time; a fight against terrorism is plainly such a project. Its goals must incorporate choices that will be desirable and accepted over that long period. Empowering the executive at the expense of the legislature and overriding particular democratic liberties that have become traditional might have been fine, and accepted, for the four years of World War II. But if these were to be the practices of decades of a war on terrorism, the country's democracy would change fundamentally. On the other hand, the long duration of the problem of terrorism means that capacities that are more difficult to create quickly can be put into place. The same is true of alliances, treaties, and other critically important forms of support among nations.

We need plans for dealing with the ups and downs of a wider variety of the forms of terrorism over the long haul. The first question is whether it helps to approach that need as if what we face is a "war."

Chapter 2

Does It Help to Define Our Dangers from Terrorism as "War"?

For a coherent, long-term strategy of dealing with terrorism after September 11, we need goals that will elicit support at home and abroad over the long term, goals that are clear enough to give some direction to the actions we take and define the capacities we should be building. Governmental goals are always a mixture of activities and objectives designed to meet a demanding need, an awareness of the limitations posed by a variety of costs, and expressive themes that relate the need and the means to widely shared motivations, thereby justifying and inspiring the undertaking.

An expressive theme is not enough. A goal and the strategy needed to implement it must be intimately related to the problem or need that requires governmental response; it requires more critical thought than simply the announcement of a public theme like "making war on terrorism." "War" is neither a persuasive description of the situation we face nor an adequate statement of our objectives. It misleads us as to the means that we will have to use. It provides undeserved dignity to our opponents. Yet we have not been given a better description of our goals.

War as a Description of the Situation We Confront

Surprisingly, the term "war" is without real definition in either the law of the United States or the law of nations. In the last half-century declarations of war have become obsolete—despite major hostilities in Korea, Vietnam, Iraq, and Afghanistan. There has been an increasing international tendency to prohibit war as an instrument of policy. Article 2 of the Charter of the United Nations forbids "the threat or use of force against the territorial integrity or political independence of any state."[1] The treaties providing protection of prisoners and other victims of "war" substitute other terms for situations in which military force is used by nations. The Geneva Conventions, specifying the rules of armed conflict, apply not only "to all cases of declared war" but as well to "any other armed conflict" between parties.[2]

In the law of the United States, the powers and other legal consequences that accompany a finding of "war" have determined judicial interpretation of what "war" means. It means different things in different contexts. During the Korean War, the Supreme Court denied President Truman the powers of a wartime commander to seize the steel mills.[3] At the same time, the Court of Military Appeals found that there was a "war" for purposes of increasing the penalty when a sentry slept on duty.[4] It may well be that the situation after September 11 legally justifies military tribunals to try members of Al Qaeda arrested in Pakistan but is too far from war to allow their use against an American arrested in Chicago.

With the minor exception of some ambiguity about the status of our conflict with the Barbary pirates early in the 1800s,[5] "war" has always required a conflict between nation-states. But we have used "war" metaphorically to indicate any relatively massive commitment of attention, energy, and resources to a dangerous problem. Thus we have committed ourselves, in the last half-century, to "wars" on poverty, crime, and drugs.

Real wars had many characteristics that even the "war on drugs" lacked. They presented overriding national objectives compared to any other domestic and foreign policy. They were led institutionally by the military, which had the central burden of responsibility. They were against a nation, which could draft soldiers and raise revenues and thus activate far greater resources than even the largest drug cartel. The enemy's objective required it to defeat our military, so often the stakes included the danger of our falling under foreign control. Such a danger was too massive and too pressing for governance with normal separation of powers. The commander in chief's vision had to be respected; national disagreement about means was too risky, and delay for legislative or public debate, too costly.

Perhaps most important, modern wars have always been temporary states—not states of prolonged, even indefinite, duration. Only that limited duration would permit a national domestic and foreign policy with a single overriding objective. Only a limited duration would permit the safe transfer of massive powers into the hands of the executive.

Although these traditional characteristics of the term "war" do not fit comfortably with its use to describe the aftermath of the attacks of September 11, that does not preclude stretching the concept if that has desirable consequences. After all, we were attacked by an organization, Al Qaeda, that seemed far larger and far better financed than the terrorist groups we and our allies had faced in the past. It displayed a ruthless willingness to kill American citizens, officials, and military for its purposes. Our responses have to be commensurate with this new degree of danger. We would find it useful to have a term that captured the danger and the need for action we may now face—something an order of magnitude more dangerous than the terrorism we had associated with such events as a handful of gunmen seizing a plane or embassy, shooting up an airport, or setting off a conventional bomb.

Providing the term "war" as a compact and familiar definition of the entirely novel situation we face after September 11 has been useful for some purposes, yet, as I will show, dangerous in the longer run. It is in these pragmatic terms that we must judge the administration's call to "war." Before we decide to let the term "war" play a big role in shaping our policies, we should compare the uses and dangers of this description of our situation after September 11 with another description: that we now face a far wider and sometimes far more dangerous range of terrorist threats than we had previously been prepared to address.

We have, in fact, discovered that there is a set of quite different activities that could be arrayed under the traditional term "terrorism." The activities range from (a) attention-getting but purposely limited violence by a small group; to (b) a continuing campaign of such violence, such as France had experienced in 1985 and 1995 and as has characterized the attacks on Israel at the beginning of the twenty-first century; to (c) the relatively spectacular attempts to kill many Americans that we have experienced in Lebanon, Saudi Arabia, Kenya and Tanzania, Oklahoma City, Washington, and New York; and finally to (d) the danger of terrorists' use of weapons of mass destruction that would increase the risk to life by another order of magnitude over the vast increase that came at "(c)" with the mere objective of massive killing. That set of forms of terrorism creates a complicated mix.

Emphasizing the rich variety of terrorism we face, rather than assimilating it all into a single category with which we are at "war," does not amount to arguing that our criminal law system, which was more than adequate to deal with small groups of terrorists in the United States, is adequate to handle Al Qaeda without the help of intelligence, foreign policy, and the military. Both descriptions of what we face recognize the need for a fuller range of capacities to deal with a more and more dangerous range of terrorism. The choice between them is pragmatic: is describing our new situation simply as "war" as helpful as acknowledging that it is a set of dangers, some of which are very serious but none of which is much like "war" in its demands on our energies and ingenuity?

Since the choice of how to define our situation is pragmatic, it is not helpful to argue as to what we can and should do from the *assumption* that we are at war. Whether we are "at war" or challenged by a new array of terrorist tactics and groups is a question of choice. We can and must decide how to define the situation.

Our Goals and Strategy Must Reflect the Complexity and the Uncertainty of the Threat

Our relatively traditional form of war against the Taliban government of Afghanistan ended when the Taliban were replaced by a friendly, allied government. The same was true of our war against Iraq's regime headed by Saddam Hussein. That in each case there was thereafter no nation against whom we were in an armed conflict does not mean that we could not extend the use of the word "war" to describe the continuing risks of terrorism, if that proved more useful than obfuscating. But obfuscation would be inevitable if the administration refused to clarify with whom we were at war. Besides the variety of forms of terrorist attack, we might be dealing with any or all of several enemies, and what we should do also depends on which of these enemies we are addressing.

If the enemy is, as CIA Director George Tenet suggested in 2002,[6] the remains of a well-organized Al Qaeda, which has trained thousands of terrorist followers, we must prevent Al Qaeda from finding a home in any nation—a step our military accomplished effectively in Afghanistan. If the enemy is those infected with hostility to the United States in much of the Muslim world (suggested by figures like 95 percent of well-educated Saudis supporting Bin Laden's cause),[7] our strategy requires a combination of short-term cooperation with foreign intelligence agencies and, equally important, longer-run efforts to create a different attitude toward the United States.

If our enemy is any *state* willing to use terrorists to attack U.S. civilians for political purposes, the threat of a U.S. military response is critical. If it is any private group, however small, willing to attack us in this way, we must recognize that the problem is a little like the problem of drug-dealing; we must try very hard to stop the activity, but also learn that we will have to live with it. Attacking harboring nations will still be important, but it will prove inadequate in light of the sobering fact that terrorist groups, like organized crime groups, have been able to work around the world without the tolerance, let alone support, of the government where they are located.

If our gravest danger flows from the rapid spread to more and smaller groups of the technology for, and willingness to use, weapons of mass destruction, we have to focus on blocking the ways these groups can get their hands on those weapons.[8]

If the enemy is all those groups using even conventional terrorist tactics against anyone in the world, not necessarily against us—if we really intend a war on all terror or on all terror with a global reach—our response in most cases cannot, realistically, be more than diplomatic support for the victim state.

Each of these possible enemies requires a different strategy. Even the most dangerous, the threat of the spread of weapons of mass destruction to many terrorist organizations, does not seem particularly responsive to military or war-like measures. Our gravest dangers from nuclear terrorists may well flow from the fact that enriched uranium or even nuclear weapons may be illegally sold or poorly guarded in, say, Russia or Pakistan.[9] Then the language of "war" would serve us poorly; for what we need is a structure of incentives and prohibitions in cooperation with these countries. The danger from biological and chemical weapons can be greatly increased by ready availability of information about such weapons on the Internet, or the selfishness of pharmaceutical companies.[10] Dealing with these threats requires multilateral treaties. Again, thinking of ourselves as making "war on terrorism" leads us in the wrong direction. Dealing with these risks requires extensive international cooperation. War does not help.

Turning to the danger from the use of conventional weapons, we might well expect the danger to come not from any single organization like Al Qaeda, against which we can sometimes use the military, but from the desire of very large numbers of individuals in Muslim countries to punish what they see as our indifference or contempt toward them, to deflate our pride and grandeur, and to reduce awe at our power by showing that we are vulnerable to terrorist attacks. Defeating the armies of the Taliban and Saddam Hussein may aggravate this threat.

With appeals to those hopes, Bin Laden may have wanted, above all else, to unite under his leadership a significant fraction of the Muslim population, making it a force to be reckoned with. The polls show an extraordinary breadth of such feelings within Arab populations and even beyond (in areas where religion has nothing to do with the motivation);[11] the waiting line to be a Palestinian suicide bomber shows the depth and breadth of commitment at the bulging extreme of the very broad spectrum of levels of support.

If this is true, then Bin Laden would be only one of many who could fan those feelings into flamboyant terrorism against the United States. In the long and medium terms, we must try to reduce, by explanations or actions, the sea of individuals whose felt grievances led to enthusiasm for Bin Laden's attacks. Our eventual safety would require a relatively widespread belief that the Muslim future lies in reformed governments and economies and that those possibilities are in their hands, not blocked, controlled, or frustrated by the United States or its allies in the area. Fostering that belief may involve loosening ties to corrupt allies even though that would be dangerous in the short run. In the medium term we will need to seek as wide agreement as possible that political violence against civilians by anyone—states or their opponents—is so unfair and cruel as to be condemned by most of the world, hoping to reduce support for *any* cause that relies on political violence against civilians. We must show that attacks on civilians are likely to alienate possible supporters of the attackers' goals, and are unlikely to affect in any major way U.S. policies or the economic, political, and military stature of the United States.[12]

Indeed, figuring out the extent of the danger—not just its source or the form it takes—is important if we are to decide what must be "paid" for security. To assess the extent of danger we must divide the risks we face from terrorism, whatever their source or motivation, into the four separate categories already described: the terrible risk of terrorist attack with a biological or nuclear weapon; the grave risk of large-scale, spectacular attacks with "conventional" weapons as on September 11; the demoralization a prolonged campaign of small-scale attacks can cause; and the far more familiar, less dangerous, forms of attack such as were common in Israel before the intifada and were once common in Northern Ireland. We must be prepared to spend more and plan more comprehensively to deal with the more dangerous forms of attack, where the cost to us might be thousands of times the cost of a familiar terrorist attack. But if they are all part of the same "war" against the same enemy ("terrorism with a global reach"), we are less likely to develop different remedies for different dangers.

The other reason for making distinctions in the source and scope of the danger is so we can be realistic about success. Because Al Qaeda has in the past spaced its attacks many months apart, we should not quickly assume that anything we did prevented a prompt repeat of the last attack. But preventing massive attacks would be an immense success that should not be overlooked even if, like France, Israel, or Northern Ireland, we become the target at home or abroad of a spate of small-scale bombers, many of whom may be suicidal. A suicide bomber bypassing the streets of Jerusalem for the streets of Los Angeles should not be treated like a threat of immense proportions, and his success in causing casualties should not be considered a defeat for our homeland defense. Above all, it should not be treated as a heartening triumph for terrorism. That would make heroes of the terrorists, greatly encourage terrorism, and cause needless disruption of our national life and confidence.

In short, each of four or more opponents is our possible enemy and each of these could engage in traditional terrorism, or a campaign of terrorism, or spectacular terrorism, or an effort to use weapons of mass destruction. To talk of "war" without recognizing these variations merely obscures the problem.

Worse, talk about "war" also obscures the level of our uncertainty about the threat we face or are likely to face. Speaking of a "war" initiated by terrorists on September 11 suggests that we somehow know the enemy and the scope of the danger he poses. In fact, one of the critical, defining characteristics of the situation we now face is its very uncertainty. A large part of our problem is how to prepare intelligently despite our uncertainty about the terrorist's motivations, organization, resources, and plans.

The American people are wise enough to recognize that, until we know more, it is sensible for a wealthy, powerful country to assume the worst even while knowing that our enemies may not be as numerous, organized, or competent as we fear. The American people recognize that we still don't know how many people willing and ready to take terrorist actions are out there; how professionally they are organized and managed; and whether they are generally as capable as the attacks on September 11 suggested or as clumsy as Richard Reid's attempt to set off his shoe bomb was. Until we start to learn more, we must be more open to change than a suggestion that we are at "war" with an identified enemy—terrorism with an international reach—suggests.

These pragmatic weaknesses in the use of "war" to describe our choices and to sustain our efforts are supplemented by the benefits the concept can offer our opponents. An undefined war on terrorism will look like a return of the Crusades to many Muslims.[13] Even if it is plainly addressed to a particular organization, Al Qaeda, it grants that organization the dignity of parity with the United States and spares it the condemnation that the terms "terrorism" and "crime" evoke. There is something heroic about being at war with the world's only super-power, as the Arabic coverage of the Iraq war showed. In Northern Ireland, members of the IRA starved themselves to death to press their demands that they be treated as prisoners of "war" rather than as common criminals.[14]

"War" and the Dangers of Reliance on the Wrong Resources

Finally, a definition of the situation we face as "war" strongly suggests that our primary reliance will continue to be on military force, even after our military victories in Afghanistan and Iraq. If use of the military was in fact the most promising avenue to deal with the variety of forms of terrorism that threaten us, there would be nothing affirmatively misleading (although nothing very helpful) about describing the situation we face as "war." The danger is that, for several reasons, the use of the term "war" points us in the wrong direction. The very term suggests a primacy for military force; that's what war has always been about. The military is the group to whom we have generally turned in situations of grave danger from hostile forces. In that sense, we may be captives of the dictum that "to a man with a hammer, everything looks like a nail." Finally, the military, recognizing the vulnerabilities of its traditional strategies for fighting wars to what it calls "asymmetrical threats," has invested its pride in efforts to meet such low-level threats. But a little thought reveals sharp limits on the usefulness of military force against terrorists sheltered by a sympathetic population or even against a state harboring terrorists.

Ultimately, success against secretive, violent terrorist groups requires either denying all who *might* fit into this category access to targets and the resources they need for particular attacks (for example, fissile materials), or identifying the potential terrorists in advance and blocking their plans in any of a variety of ways, from arrest or detention of the suspects to disruption or frustration of their actions by asset-freezing or seizure. Either of these ways of preventing terrorism can take place within the United States or abroad, and can be carried out either by Americans or by officials of a friendly nation. In this complex of possibilities, the military has an important but distinctly limited role.

Abroad, the military should and will provide much of the protection against terrorist attacks on U.S. installations. U.S. citizens abroad will necessarily continue to rely, for ordinary policing, on foreign police forces. The critical activity abroad, where terrorist groups can hope to plan, recruit, supply, and finance their operations against the U.S. mainland more safely than they could within U.S. borders, is intelligence-gathering. That requires human sources, and close-in electronic and physical surveillance, not advanced military technology. The critical capacities—ability to recruit agents that not only can speak the language, but can also pass easily in the communities that terrorists share with supporters—are largely in the hands of foreign intelligence agencies and our CIA. Building a separate military capability here is hard to justify.

Our military capacities may well be critical in reminding other nations of the lessons of Afghanistan under the Taliban and Iraq under Hussein. We will not tolerate a hostile nation providing even a haven to a group planning, training, financing, or providing needed resources for attacks on the United States or its people and property abroad. We will not risk a hostile nation delivering weapons of mass destruction to terrorists. We can even try to impose a requirement of cooperation by broadening our threat to include states that fail to cooperate in good faith with our efforts to find and disable such groups or disable such activities.

But even in this area, there are distinct limits to what the military can accomplish. Some states will lack the competence to really help and other states that do not believe in our cause or fear terrorist retaliation will make efforts too half-hearted to be effective but real enough to be indistinguishable from unpunishable incompetence. Both may remind us that we were unable to detect terrorist preparations in the United States that went on for years before September 11, and that Britain, France, Germany, and Italy have all had similar problems. There's the rub. What will we do when a state where terrorists may be planning attacks on us claims it cannot find them or when a state with weapons of mass destruction or needed technology or ingredients loses count or control of them?[15] For then any attack will threaten the continued support of our coalition and cause widespread suspicion of injustice within the United States.

To assure good faith and to create competent local law enforcement, we could demand access for our investigators or even military forces to conduct law enforcement operations in such places as Iran, Syria, Libya, Sudan, or Somalia, but these states are not likely to agree to that sacrifice of sovereignty. Even Saudi Arabia would not allow the FBI to freely investigate the bombing of the Khobar Towers.[16] Even if all agreed, the capacity of U.S. soldiers or investigators to find terrorists in an unfriendly setting, without taking over the country, is likely to be very low indeed. Our experience pursuing Al Qaeda leaders in Afghanistan is not heartening.

How serious is this problem—this limit to our effective reach? That depends on how many of the terrorist organizations that threaten our security depend upon relatively open tolerance by the states where they prepare for terrorism and how many can operate at a lower, far less conspicuous, level of support. One possibility is that the group's preparations for terrorism require the active support or at least the open tolerance of a particular state. That is, it may need relatively open havens for recruiting, supplying, and planning and maybe additional state resources. A second possibility—suggested by the history of the IRA or the Basque ETA or Colombia's FARC terrorists—is that the terrorist group works more like organized crime; i.e., that it is not willingly tolerated by the state where it is found, but is able to operate (and cooperate with other such groups) through secrecy, corruption, and intimidation.

Even for terrorist organizations in the first category, where state support or tolerance is now available and open, the threat of war with the United States and other states that align themselves with us, or of extreme economic sanctions, may not cut off what the organization needs. First, the support may continue but in a more carefully concealed form, as many believe happened after we bombed Libya in 1985 in retaliation for its terrorism against U.S. soldiers in Berlin. Similarly, we suspected, but could not prove until after the fall of the Communist states in Eastern Europe, that they were providing support for various terrorist groups in the West. Second, the terrorist organization whose support by one state is withdrawn may find alternative support in another state that is unrelentingly hostile to the United States and prepared to bear the consequences. Finally, some terrorist organizations now working with the support or tolerance of a state can and will shift into the second "organized crime" category, operating without state support.

Terrorist organizations that operate like organized crime groups without the support or willing tolerance of a state can be affected by U.S. efforts only in two situations. First, the United States can insist on helping the unwilling host to create the capability to deal with any terrorist group using its territory to prepare for terrorism abroad. Looking at our attempts to improve the state capability to fight drug lords in places such as Mexico and Colombia does not provide great reassurance. There are some successes but many failures. Alternatively, the United States can go in with its own forces and try to deal with a terrorist group that is not actively supported or openly tolerated by a state but cannot be controlled by it. But that would be taken as a frightening invasion of sovereignty.

After action against Afghanistan, then, there are limited prospects of substantial results from military threats or actions to reduce terrorism rooted in a state too incompetent or unenthusiastic to pursue the terrorists—perhaps because they do not threaten its own territory. Open support or tolerance by a state and any advantages to a terrorist group that depends on such open acceptance can be denied by threat of force or economic sanctions. But what will remain, unless hearts and minds are converted, are secret support and tolerance, often hidden behind a claim of lack of capacity to find the group or detect its preparations. And we have no military remedy for these. Nor is the prospect of direct military attack on terrorists hidden in a sympathetic population much better without recourse to unacceptable repression.

In the end, we need a level of willing and competent cooperation abroad that we cannot effectively compel. That limits the usefulness of military force and requires persuasion and developing partnerships at the working level—a lesson the Israelis have now learned painfully. Our objective has to be a new international norm against terrorism that is broadly and sincerely based, not because international norms are gentler and fuzzier than missiles and bullets but because only dedicated host-nation cooperation will work.

The limited role of the military is even clearer when we are considering the activities at home designed for the same two purposes: to restrict access to targets and dangerous resources to those whose access is not dangerous; and to gather intelligence about those who may be dangerous so that we can monitor and then disrupt their plans. We do not need the military to replace the Secret Service and the Department of Homeland Security or to protect the Congress. Within the United States we do not need the military to guard most facilities that are likely to be targets of terrorist attacks, nor do we need the military to gather the secrets that can disarm dangerous terrorists and defeat their plans.

In fact, we have a tradition going back well over a century of keeping the military out of domestic law enforcement, both because it is trained for war and not policing, and because we fear the centralization of power that would come with domestic control managed by the commander in chief or the secretary of defense. We also have a tradition since the 1970s of keeping the Defense Department out of intelligence-gathering about domestic activities, and that tradition has served well both the military (by preserving public respect) and the public (by providing more confidence in the privacy of political activities).

Part II

What Can Be Done to Reduce the Threat?

Chapter 3

Protection against Unidentified Terrorists

In the following two chapters, I will review what we can do to prevent terrorist attacks. The first set of possibilities, explored in this chapter, does not require a state to know in advance which individuals or groups threaten it. Even without that information, a state can attempt to restrict access to targets and resources and try to reduce the grievances that motivate terrorist recruits.

Chapter 4 addresses the two promising possibilities that turn upon either gathering intelligence in advance of a terrorist attack with the purpose of disrupting the terrorists' plans by detention, imprisonment, seizing assets, or other means; or, alternatively, successfully discovering after the fact who was responsible for an attack and taking steps specifically to deter that group and more generally to deter others who will fear being identified and punished.

Creating a Framework

Through these two chapters, my effort will be to develop as complete a menu as possible of ways to recreate safety and reduce fear. Stated differently, the question is: if it is not to be the military and war, then how might we defend ourselves? A menu of options is not, of course, the whole story. What will work depends on how the menu of possibilities relates to the motivations and the resources of the terrorists and to the situations in which the options might be used. For example, knowing which targets to protect depends on knowing something about the motivations of the terrorists; and knowing where we want to spend resources to guard dangerous materials depends upon knowing how feasible that denial of access is in light of their present availability (e.g., anthrax) or unavailability (e.g., enriched uranium) in the world. Whether to adopt a particular option, even if it looks promising in light of the motivation of the terrorists and the situation in which they are working, also depends on whether its cost, not only in dollars and American lives, but also in terms of our values, exceeds its benefits. Even one concerned solely with preventing terrorism would recognize that making that judgment well determines how far American citizens, our allies, and those suspicious of us can accept what we are doing as right or necessary.

That said, the fact remains that for the United States, the world has changed dramatically since September 11, 2001. We no longer feel secure, although we cannot measure the extent of the danger. Nothing is more important to us than reestablishing the reality and sense of security. In the meantime, being less secure means that we have to take a variety of steps to reestablish safety. Some of those steps involve reducing the harmful consequences of any attack; some involve the psychological sense of enhanced security and autonomy that comes with effective retaliation. Our focus here is on something more fundamental than either of these: what are the possibilities for stopping successful attacks by international terrorists in the United States? Since not all terrorism poses the same threat, my focus here is on the most dangerous forms: what can be done to stop any sustained campaign of quite lethal terrorism, to prevent "spectaculars," and to reduce the danger of weapons of mass destruction. That and not the more familiar problem of reducing occasional, low-level terrorism is the subject of this and the following chapter.

Among the possibilities there are several critical distinctions. Most important by far, protective actions can be taken at home and thus within U.S. control, or they can be taken abroad. Terrorists from abroad will presumably appear in the United States, their target country, in fewer numbers and for shorter periods. Abroad in their home base they need a more permanent organization to provide planning, training, and financing. That gives a distinct advantage to any investigation abroad, all else being equal.

All else is never equal. The second closely related distinction is whether the protective action will be taken by U.S. officials or will require cooperative action by foreign intelligence, law enforcement, or military. Extra-territorial criminal statutes have allowed the FBI to investigate terrorism abroad, with the consent of the host government. And the CIA can recruit agents abroad. Somewhat offsetting these advantages of taking action ourselves is the far greater knowledge a cooperative government is likely to have of what is occurring within its borders. Moreover, to the extent that the terrorists operate from a non-democratic haven abroad, they are potentially subject to a dictator's control over a state internal security apparatus that uses techniques that the United States would not tolerate at home.

A third critical distinction is the one separating this chapter from the one that follows: whether the option we use does or does not require us to learn in advance which terrorists are planning attacks. The distinction is not always sharp or comfortable. Gathering intelligence about future attacks by monitoring who is seeking access to targets or resources deters unidentified perpetrators and is also closely related to later efforts to assure that only trustworthy people have such access. The prospect of attributing responsibility that gives credibility to deterrent threats against individuals, groups, or states depends upon intelligence that has been gathered before as well as after an attack.

Each of the five likely categories for preventing a terrorist attack are identified vertically as rows 1–5 on Figure 3.1.

TERRORIST NEEDS

STATE PREVENTIVE STRATEGIES	A. Recruits and continuing members	B. Resources	C. Training	D. Tactical information	E. Access	F. Means to escape	G. A haven	H. Hope	I. Social acceptance a. by terrorist organization b. by wider support network
1. Reducing enthusiasm for attacks on the United States									
2. Deterrence through law enforcement, military, or economic threats against: a. individuals b. groups c. states									
3. Denying access to: a. targets b. resources c. the United States									
4. Gathering and processing information (intelligence) on individuals, groups, organizations, and activities									
5. Disruption including asset forfeiture and incapacitation through: a. criminal prosecution b. detention									

Figure 3.1 The Logic of Prevention

The first three—discouraging recruits, deterring terrorists by threatening retaliation, and denying access to targets and resources—can be taken without advance knowledge of the terrorists' plans. The last—disrupting the activities of terrorists by everything from seizing their funds or disarming their weapons to misleading or detaining them—depends upon the fourth, gathering and processing information. These last two categories of prevention are the subject of Chapter 4.

A good way of both checking the adequacy of these five categories and of enriching them by adding specific possibilities to each category is to imagine what terrorists need and how we can disrupt their meeting their needs. The column headings A–I on the chart in Figure 3.1 reflect the needs of a terrorist group, based abroad, which is planning large-scale attacks on U.S. targets. Creating the columns and rows on the chart and then filling in the boxes at each intersection breaks the difficult task of imagining the full range of moves and countermoves into two more manageable parts. The first is an expandable, amendable list of what a terrorist group might need to mount a sustained campaign of terrorist attacks on the United States. The second is imagining what the United States or supportive nations can do to interfere with each of those steps.

Applying the Framework

Take, first, the column headings. To accomplish such a campaign, a terrorist organization must (1) have a flow of recruits and the capacity to retain members' commitment and loyalty. That in turn requires (a) hope for the desired results of terrorism; (b) approval by valued members of the organization as well as by a wider social network; and (c) some prospect of a range of personal rewards from the honor of martyrdom to live leadership status—requirements described on the chart in columns H and I. (2) The terrorist organization must be able to provide recruits with the resources—including financing and weapons—needed to attack a target. (3) It must train them in the variety of skills (organizational, technical, tactical, etc.) that executing a sustained terrorist campaign requires. (4) It needs tactical information about the target and its protection. (5) The organization must furnish its operatives a means of getting access to the target for those carrying out the operation and for their chosen weapons. (6) Unless suicide is part of the plan, they must have a means of escaping both the devastation they cause and their pursuers. (7) All of this is likely to depend upon creating and maintaining an enduring organization and managing it without the open or discoverable support of a state against which the United States may retaliate and despite any effort by a host state to dismantle it. As noted, the morale necessary to sustain the organization over years requires both (8) hope and (9) internal and external social and psychological support.[1] Many of these conditions can be best met abroad. Almost all must be accomplished in secrecy (or some of them with the secret tolerance of those who might otherwise prevent them) despite the intelligence efforts of both the United States and its allies. All require organizational leadership, too.

As to each of these requirements we should ask: what makes it easier and what could make it more difficult for a terrorist group to accomplish that step and what capacity is available to us to affect either? The answers not only provide our options but also permit a rough estimate of the limits of the effectiveness of each option alone and all options together.

Reducing enthusiasm for attacks on the United States

Whether our "enemy" is a hierarchical organization or a foundation-like group or a number of small groups sensing a shared grievance against the United States, reducing enthusiasm for attacking the United States is a long-run aim of immense importance. If we have to fear attacks by small groups sharing more in the way of grievances than in the way of organization, reducing enthusiasm for attacking the United States becomes essential, not just important. The rewards of reducing the total number of potential recruits available as activists or supporters of potential attacks are more than great enough to justify the attempt. Still, the problems are imposing.

If even a tenth of 1 percent of the Muslim population or of the quarter of that that is Arab is heavily motivated to support a sustained campaign of terrorism, any steps we take to reduce that number would have to be remarkably effective. Even if we were able to cut that category by 75 percent or 95 percent, the remaining 25 percent or 5 percent would be able to subject us to much the same dangers as before. Moreover, the steps we take to reduce enthusiasm for attacking us would have to reach all the way to the most angry and hostile fringe of the population that feels aggrieved and in need of heroes.

This assumes, as we often do, that our danger flows from a discrete, angry group largely unaffected and unsupported by the views and attitudes of a far larger population among whom they live. The more optimistic model is the opposite. Then we could have an impact on terrorism by reducing the enthusiasm of those who might otherwise have been supporters or tacit supporters of the terrorists, relying on their attitudes and actions to, in turn, reduce terrorism.

The possibilities of action in this category are limited. Distinguishing among four is clarifying. We can attempt to improve the conditions of the aggrieved. We can attempt to dispel the idea that we are responsible for the conditions that cause grievances. We can encourage more revulsion at attacks on civilian populations. We can try to show that terrorism does not advance the causes of the terrorists.

The most difficult way to accomplish our goal is to change the conditions that cause grievances. We do not know either the causal or the preventive relationship between felt grievances and terrorist actions. We do not even know the relationship between changed activities on our part and, first, an improvement in conditions abroad and, then, a reduction in grievances against the United States. Moreover, the changes that seem most promising in reducing grievances bear heavy costs. Economically, it would take vast sums to change the living conditions of the average Muslim citizen abroad.[2] The case for U.S. economic assistance to oil-rich states will never be compelling where some redistribution of the present wealth combined with efforts to reduce the rate of population growth could do as much or more.

Politically, if we strongly support the creation of truly democratic regimes in Muslim countries, none of which now exist, we may lose the needed assistance of their present undemocratic governments in our efforts to thwart terrorism. We will surely be seen by those governments, if not their citizens, as meddling impermissibly in their internal affairs.

Changing foreign or military policies is hardly more promising. Whether we remove our troops from the Arab world—another Al Qaeda demand—must depend largely on the need for them to be there to protect allies. Our support for Israel may represent proof of our hostility to many Arabs, encouraging support for Palestinian organizations related to Al Qaeda or its successors. Still our position with regard to the Palestinian intifada and the Israeli response has to depend on our relationships with the immediate parties, our opinions of the legitimacy of their actions, and the long-term consequences of either deserting allies or allowing terrorism to triumph. Having recognized all this by way of caution, we have little to lose and much to gain by showing concern for the well-being—the nutrition, health, education, governance, and human rights—of Muslim populations around the world.

This is not the only way we can try to affect the pool of possible recruits to, and supporters of, terrorism. By actions such as those just described or by influencing information flows, we can try to prevent the attribution to U.S. purposes of whatever causes the anger and despair in much of the Muslim world. After all, we are not the cause of poverty, sickness, lack of education, governmental corruption and incompetence, and failures of justice and democracy in much of the Arab or broader Muslim world. As the world's only superpower, however—economically, diplomatically, and militarily—we are a highly attractive explanation for the conspiratorially minded. Indeed, it is in the interest even of governments we have long regarded as "friendly" to allow the causes of popular grievances to be attributed to the United States.

Thus, besides showing U.S. concern for the welfare of Muslims throughout the world, we must take steps to attack efforts to use us as a scapegoat. Intangible grounds for resentment—the sense of hopelessness, political impotence, and the feeling of being left behind in a modern world—will be the hardest to show are not the fault of the United States; for they are generated to a significant extent by our very power and wealth, however they are used. Affirmatively, we must show that there is a path to dignity, respect, and progress for Muslims who lack those immensely important goods now; and we must show that the path doesn't run through attacks on the United States. To show that a path to dignity, respect, and progress doesn't start with attacks on us, we have to be careful not to reward, by concession or status, such attacks. To show that there is another path to these goods, we must make clear that the real prospects for human and economic development lie in dedicated, efficient, patriotic self-government. Inevitably, that will cause us to point out that some of our closest allies represent the real obstacles to the progress of their people. This will put us in conflict with governments that might therefore be less willing to support our efforts against terrorists among their people. Perhaps worse, it might require us to risk elections that might be won by those who hate us. These consequences can be delayed, but not forever. The only way to end terrorism will be to show that it is the wrong direction to go in a search for hope, health, dignity, and wealth.

Of course, we should also be attempting to discourage any systematic efforts to purvey hostile views of the United States.

Our allies, the Saudis and the Pakistanis, have broadly supported schools encouraging hatred of non-Muslims and often terrorism.[3] Even media sources that are regularly denied the freedom to question their own government are allowed to attack us in slanderous ways.[4] We can demand more of friendly governments.

Indeed, a private cable channel in California has begun bringing to the United States in translation first-hand knowledge of the Islamist messages being broadcast in the Middle East. This will automatically generate U.S. public pressure on these governments at the same time as it educates us. In part, the problem is with our own credibility. We must find ways to establish sources of information, even about matters as incontestable as responsibility for the September 11 attacks, which have almost unimpeachable integrity among many of those most skeptical about the goodwill of the United States.

By a combination of (a) demanding consideration of human rights in our own actions and in those of our allies, and (b) explaining in vivid ways the horror of attacks on civilians, including children, we can also attempt to make terrorism illegitimate in the minds of enough supporters of the terrorist cause to discourage that tactic. Inspiring pictures of the "martyrs" who have engaged in suicide bombings are available in much of the Muslim world. We should try to make equally available, after a terrorist attack, pictures of the babies without limbs, children without parents, and grieving loved ones.

The benefits of creating revulsion at attacks on civilians can be great, but only if we assume that the steps we and our allies take do not appear, even to the suspicious, as morally equivalent to the terrorism. That requires sometimes costly restraint in terms of military response and in the use of law enforcement and intelligence agencies abroad and at home. Our campaign in Iraq in 2003 was designed with the benefits of such restraint in mind.

CREATING DISINCENTIVES THROUGH DETERRENCE

An alternative way of reducing the enthusiasm of individuals for attacking the United States is to create disincentives, i.e., by deterrence. The wisest observers of terrorist activity are skeptical about the effectiveness of deterring individual terrorists, although it is well worth the costs of trying.[5] It is doubtful whether the limited U.S. ability to capture and detain or try terrorists will provide much disincentive to recruitment, particularly among the sizeable number of highly motivated volunteers, with widespread support among their local communities. A critical part of deterrence of crime within a nation is the social condemnation that accompanies punishment. That factor is simply not present for foreign-based terrorists. And even for a non-suicidal terrorist, the United States can hardly increase the already severe sanctions he faces if caught. Increasing deterrence would require increasing the chance of apprehension, an increase of risk that may hardly be noticed by the most motivated fringe of any passionate movement. A more promising possibility is that, as with crime in American cities in the 1990s, the convincing sense that an attack can work (which may have made plans for the attack on September 11, 2001, look particularly tempting) changes with massive efforts to catch and punish terrorists.

This dismal picture of the prospects of deterrence of individual terrorists could be brightened by adopting a scheme that systematically punishes terrorism—not the individual terrorist—by harming the terrorist cause with the adoption of retaliatory policies, e.g., giving additional military, economic, or diplomatic support to the traditional enemies of the terrorist group. Even the most dedicated and zealous terrorist may forgo terrorism if his actions could harm his "cause." But the cost of deterring in this way is the adoption of policies that may otherwise not be desirable.

In particular, with this form of sanction, as with many other steps, the benefits of deterrence may be bought at the price of increasing the motivating enthusiasm of other potential terrorists at the same time. Each of the deterrent steps that we could take has the potential of costly side effects that must be considered. Assassinations incapacitate, disrupt, and deter, but they also create martyrs and thus stimulate imitation, as Israel has learned in the Palestinian territories. Any effort to use changed policies as a deterrent provides "new evidence" of hostility, the effect of which in reinforcing hatred may overwhelm any deterrent effect.

The same is true of any change that suggests institutional unfairness, such as the early searches by the British of Catholic homes in Northern Ireland.[6] The problem is not limited to deterrence, of course. Even reducing grievances can have its costs in terms of encouraging terrorism. Making things better *after* a terrorist event has taken place or been threatened may look to potential recruits as a victory or reward to those leaders who threaten terrorism. Prime Minister Ehud Barak's abrupt withdrawal in 2000 of Israeli troops under attack by Hezbollah in Lebanon provided what appeared to be a "lesson" to Hamas.[7]

As Ariel Merari, one of Israel's great terrorism experts, has pointed out, the prospects of deterrence are much stronger when the threats are addressed to states or groups.[8] States, even pre-war Iraq, respond to the threat of military, economic, or diplomatic sanctions (although the response may be merely to create the false appearance of compliance). States are not suicidal. Their leaders hope to stay in office. They fear the resentment of their own publics. This creates the capacity of the United States to demand cooperation from other governments that may not share our goals when dealing with terrorism.

Terrorist groups also want to continue in existence; their leaders want to stay in place. A threat that brings these fundamental attributes into question can well be effective, at least in changing the scope of activities of the terrorist group. Most terrorist groups, including Al Qaeda, in recent years have foregone the great benefits of claiming responsibility for their actions in order to protect themselves. This is substantial evidence that they are deterrable if they can be located and attacked without extensive damage to innocent lives and property.

Deterring terrorist groups or states responsible for their actions requires not only military force, which we have readily available, but an ability to attribute terrorist plans or attacks to the right groups or a state. Because of the evidence that a terrorist attack leaves behind, this is likely to be much easier than detecting the attack in advance. Deterring a terrorist-friendly state also requires a willingness to take hostile actions against that state. If the terrorists have found haven in a state generally friendly to the United States or in a great power whose responses we fear, the difficulties of deterrence are magnified immensely.

DENYING ACCESS TO TARGETS AND TO THE RESOURCES AND INFORMATION NECESSARY FOR ATTACKING THEM

To carry out the September 11 attacks in New York, the terrorists had to find a way to bring two huge explosives into the World Trade Center buildings. Access to the buildings from the air was uncontrolled. To get the huge explosives—the needed resources—they had only to get control of planes leaving Boston with enough fuel to take them to California. To direct the planes, they had to have at least minimal flight skills and information about navigating. To take over the controls of a plane, they needed numbers (four or five persons) and at least primitive weapons.

The possibilities for preventing the repetition of such an event, without prior knowledge about a group planning it, come directly out of this, admittedly partial, list of what the terrorists had to do. Many of these steps had to take place within the United States. The government has since taken steps to strengthen controls of access to: weapons on planes; the controls of planes (the cockpit); and even the buildings that might be targets from the air. (President Bush has authorized firing on planes that may be targeting certain buildings.)[9] It is easy enough to make the case for forbidding weapons on planes, preventing passengers from entering the pilot compartment, and prohibiting planes from flying in airspace near attractive targets. There is no legitimate and compelling need for granting general access to any of these forbidden acts or places.

The desirability of denying almost everyone access to the fissile materials essential to manufacturing a nuclear weapon is straightforward for a similar reason: there is no legitimate need for most people to possess such materials. The danger of nuclear terrorism is so great that the benefits of sharply limiting access to the fissile materials that are necessary to carry it out far exceed the costs. The critical question is how (not whether) to effectively deny access to those who would buy, steal, or pay a bribe to obtain enriched uranium or plutonium.

My colleagues Graham Allison and Ashton Carter have written much on ways to make it more difficult for would-be terrorists to obtain nuclear materials. It is enough to say here that any foreseeable expense to the United States in acquiring, destroying, or guarding materials needed for atomic weapons anywhere in the world is vastly more than justified in light of the risk they pose in terrorists' hands. Allison's argument is that our relatively extensive efforts in Russia are not nearly enough, even there.[10] Carter emphasizes that such efforts have to be extended to other nations with nuclear capabilities and must be aided by our allies.[11] Both points are indisputable.

Restricting access to targets and resources becomes more difficult when they are also used, entirely peaceably, by law-abiding citizens. Relatively few targets and resources fall into the category of the cockpit of a plane or the possession of fissile materials. The vast majority of possible targets and of available resources for attacking them are now readily available to most people and for good reasons. The targets and resources in this category are too numerous for all to be guarded.

The United States can and does control access to a relatively small percentage of the attractive targets in this category, but there are far too many to rigorously limit access to every such target whose loss might have major effects or create pervasive feelings of insecurity in the United States. Similarly, there are a large number of resources that might be useful in a terrorist attack, many more than one could sensibly guard. The problem is dramatically illustrated by the inability of Israel to protect itself against terrorist attacks by Palestinians during the second intifada. There are too many potential targets even in that small country, and both the resources (conventional explosives, nails, and other metal) and the needed information or skills (how to make a suicide bomb) are too freely available.

With too many targets and too many resources available for attacking them, those charged with our security must guess, for they cannot even monitor access to all targets and all destructive resources, let alone effectively limit access to those persons who are demonstrably safe. They must try to choose the targets we want most to protect, and also protect the targets that may be most attractive to terrorists, designing access controls for these limited categories. They also have to guess at the most dangerous resources or the ones most attractive to terrorists and try to monitor or limit access to these.

This requires capacities that the United States has not had in the past, but that both our intelligence agencies and our new Department of Homeland Security are working to develop. "Red Teaming" (asking a group of skilled and informed people to imagine what they would do if they were terrorists) can help. Tom Clancy imagined the use of airliners to attack the Capitol before September 11.[12] As Ash Carter has pointed out, home-grown computer hackers could be a big help in imagining and detecting vulnerabilities in that field.

Our capacity to guess intelligently would be considerably enhanced by increased strategic intelligence about the motivations of those who might attack us. Will they seek targets in terms of the greatest damage they can impose; or the greatest fear they can create; or the greatest enthusiasm they can generate in their own followers? What does their view of the world (e.g., a hatred of American commercialism) or the limited knowledge they may have about the United States tell us about how the particular terrorist group would apply one of those criteria? Abu Abbas used advertising brochures to pick the *Achille Lauro* as the means of infiltrating terrorists into Israel in 1985; it was the best source of information he had safely available to him.[13]

Once certain targets and resources have been identified for special protection, and once it is clear that access cannot sensibly be restricted to a very small group (as in the case of cockpits and fissile materials), a decision must be made as to the level of risk we are prepared to assume for each possible target. At one extreme, we could require the equivalent of a full security clearance for access; at the other, we could admit everyone who has not been shown by a cursory check of files to have terrorist purposes. The first would require us to make and maintain extensive records on very large numbers of Americans. The second would expose our most endangered targets and our most feared means of attacking them to grave risks. A middle way would be to insist on a reliable identity document that could be quickly checked against computerized records of known activities—files that themselves could be more or less extensive. The more valuable the target, the more reason there is to insist on something approaching a clearance procedure.

For most of the multitude of targets, it would make sense to require some reasonable and factual basis for denying access to any place that is generally open to the American public. Thus, denying an individual access, freely enjoyed by others, to a flight, or to pilot training, or to information about the World Trade Center depends upon our having a record showing that the individual poses at least a minimal risk of political violence. That leaves us, however, with the problem of "new faces," about whom no one—not even our allies—has information. Al Qaeda carefully chose such "new faces" for the September 11 attacks.

The number of potential "new faces" may be very large, and there are only a limited number of ways of dealing with the problem they pose. We could permit access only after developing a certain amount of information about the individual—enough to reduce the likelihood that he or she is a terrorist. We could permit access but monitor and record the person's activities, later checking those records against records of other activities or associations. This would use, as a deterrent, the person's knowledge that the government has records of access that can be turned to if there is an attack. Both of these alternatives could be costly; neither is particularly promising.

PROFILING

Last, we could apply one of these costly alternatives to a relatively small portion of the "new faces," based on the individual's more obvious (and cheaply identifiable) characteristics such as gender, age, country of origin, or non-citizen status. The use of more extensive checks before visas are granted to males of a certain age coming from particular Arab countries has vastly increased the government's workload and sharply increased the inconvenience to applicants since September 11. But they also permit greater reassurance that someone given access to the United States and thus to targets within the United States is not a terrorist. The same principles guide airline employees asking special questions of those in readily identified, high-risk categories who are planning to fly from an airport in the United States.

In sum, denying access to targets and resources works well when few people need to use them for legitimate purposes. But denying or controlling access to familiar places and resources is far more inconvenient to individuals and, because of the number of individuals involved, far more costly to the government. Both of these considerations suggest the desirability of imposing costly access checks on a far smaller portion of the population: those who are (a) more likely to be dangerous and (b) easily and cheaply identifiable.

The basis for identifying such people is likely to be either their religion, ethnicity, race, or nationality or a record of their prior activities. The first three raise serious ethical issues, and also can create dangerous resentments that can lead to tacit or outright support of terrorist activity. Distinguishing among alien visitors on the basis of nationality is less of a concern. The last requires checking parts of the life history of a much larger population for generally innocent activities, which when combined, are signs of potential terrorism, and keeping files that reflect the results.

Much about these possibilities is captured in Figure 3.2. The rows A–F reflect the major options for restricting access. The columns 1–6 reflect some (but not all) likely candidates as subgroups within the larger population that might be selectively subject to one of the options reflected by the six rows. We are, for example, presently subjecting males of a certain age, coming from certain Arab countries, to something between the "B" and "C" category of review. What the chart does not reflect is the decision as to what level of risk should be accepted with regard to specific targets or resources after whatever investigation is required has been carried out, or what level of risk warrants flatly denying access or monitoring access and keeping records.

The chart also does not reflect the price that selecting one of the boxes requires us to pay in two ways. First, the inevitable result is increased alienation within the group selected for special restrictions on access. There is a major impact on the sense of shared community, which determines much of an individual's security and the sense of well-being in the nation. There is an additional cost. If the experience of Israel and the United Kingdom is any indication, we are less likely to get

POSSIBLE BASIS

POSSIBLE ACTIONS	1. Everyone	2. All aliens	3. Temporary visitors	4. Resident aliens an temporary visitors from certain countries	5. Temporary visitors from certain countries	6. Members of, or contributors to (or "associated with") certain political or religious groups with certain ties to terrorism
A. Flatly denying access to all but a few who "need" access						
B. Conditioning access on a relatively full "clearance" investigation						
C. Conditioning access on a review of files, check of documents, or minor investigation						
D. Conditioning access on further checks if there is suspicious activity or a suspicious history						
E. Monitoring access and simply keeping records						
F. No check on access and no monitoring						

Figure 3.2 Alternative Ways of Denying Access to Targets and Resources

badly needed information and cooperation from many members of a group so identified as warranting suspicion.

The obvious alternative is to use the capacity of high-powered computers to combine readily available snippets of information and thereby select the subgroup whose access is to be restricted. This investigative technique as a method of screening would require a reliable way to determine the true identity of individuals seeking access to a target, an adequate and reliable fund of intelligence information to be processed to identify more risky sub-classes of the population, and an ability to cross-reference the two quickly and conveniently. Two examples, taken from the Markle Foundation Task Force report on intelligence, are:

Illustration #1: Analysts could have asked how many holders of visas from certain countries had spent more than a month in Afghanistan and then correlated those people with others who have spent time in Afghanistan to see who shares addresses, phone numbers, credit cards, or bank accounts. Such searches can and should be done in ways that reveal only the identities of the matches.

Illustration #2: Analysts could identify purchasers of airline tickets who have telephoned persons on a terrorist watch-out list during the past year.[14]

The Markle Foundation Task Force report on intelligence provided a powerful example of how this might have worked in the case of the September 11 attacks using only readily available, relatively public information.

Conclusion

The above discussion makes two critically important facts apparent. First, the activities that will be essential to prevention are very largely outside the scope of military actions and are far from ordinary conceptions of war. Rather than the

Excerpt from the Markle Foundation Task Force Report

ILLUSTRATION NO. 2: "WATCH-OUT LISTS" AND "GATES": A HYPO-THETICAL APPLICATION TO THE 9/11 ATTACKS*

Hypothesis: Each person buying an airplane ticket is checked against lists of possible terrorists. If there is a 'hit,' that person's available information is checked to identify possible associates.

• Software already exists that can check names and addresses against multiple databases. It is capable of accounting for errors and variations in the way names are spelled, and can perform these functions on very large databases in seconds.

The Application:

• In late August 2001 Nawaf Alhamzi and Khalid Al-Midhar bought tickets to fly on American Airlines Flight 77 (which was flown into the Pentagon). They bought the tickets using their real names. Both names were then on a State Department/INS watch list called TIPOFF. Both men were sought by the FBI and CIA as suspected terrorists, in part because they had been observed at a terrorist meeting in Malaysia.

• These two passenger names would have been exact matches when checked against the TIPOFF list. But that would only have been the first step. Further data checks could then have begun.

• Checking for common addresses (address information is widely available, including on the Internet), analysts would have discovered that Salem Al-Hamzi (who also bought a seat on American 77) used the same address as Nawaf Alhazmi. More importantly, they could have discovered that Mohammed Atta (American 11, North Tower of the World Trade Center) and Marwan Al-Shehhi (United 175, South Tower of the World Trade Center) used the same address as Khalid Al-Midhar.

• With Mohammed Atta now also identified as a possible associate of the wanted terrorist, Al-Midhar, analysts could have added

Atta's phone numbers (also publicly available information) to their checklist. By doing so they would have identified five other hijackers (Fayez Ahmed, Mohand Alshehri, Wail Alshehri, Waleed Alshehri, and Abdulaziz Alomari).

• With days still remaining before the scheduled flights, additional investigations could have turned up information about attendance at flight schools (information that the U.S. government then did not have in a digitally searchable form) or on puzzling foreign links (like common financial links to Hamburg, information that the government was not able to assess in real time).

• Closer to September 11, a further check of passenger lists against a more innocuous INS watch list (for expired visas) would have identified Ahmed Alghamdi. Through him, the same sort of relatively simple correlations could have led to identifying the remaining hijackers, who boarded United 93 (which crashed in Pennsylvania).

Source: Information for this illustration was drawn from work done by Systems Research & Development, one of the firms that has developed relevant software, in this case with the help of venture capital supplied by the CIA-sponsored firm, In-Q-Tel.

Defense Department, we will need the State Department, the Treasury Department, the Justice Department, the CIA, and the FBI in the long run.

The task of reducing resentment falls to international development agencies, international information programs, and diplomatic pressure on friendly nations that have been supporting schools that teach hatred toward us. All these are functions of the State Department. So is encouraging the collaboration of foreign governments in pursuing those within their borders who are planning terrorism against us.

The gathering of information about individuals known or likely to be terrorists from liaison with foreign intelligence agencies will be primarily the responsibility of the CIA. There, too, will lay the responsibility for developing our own sources of information about terrorist activities abroad—information useful in itself but also necessary to monitor the seriousness of efforts by allies on our behalf. Pursuing the terrorists moving between a number of nations will depend on the CIA as well.

Within the United States it will be the FBI, supplemented by the Homeland Security Department, which has to develop the intelligent guesses behind efforts to monitor access to targets and resources and other suspicious activities. It is these agencies that will have to process the information acquired, in light of hypotheses developed, to look for the reasonable suspicions that would justify denying access to targets or resources, or monitoring individuals and their associates. In all of this, the Defense Department does not have a central role for a simple reason: this is not war.

The second point is even more important. Hardly a step I have described as potentially effective in preventing terrorism does not have side effects that are likely either to encourage terrorism or to be costly in terms of our own democratic traditions. The latter is the subject of Chapter 5, but the former is a limit on the effectiveness of the steps we might take that has to be considered wholly aside from their costs in democratic liberties and dollars. "War" doesn't invite considering such trade-offs, but they are important for fighting terrorism.

Israel during the recent intifada again presents a dramatic example. Much of what has been done may be, to again borrow State Department jargon, "counter-productive," regardless of one's views of its morality or consistency with national traditions. In the name of war, Israel, like Britain in Northern Ireland, has sometimes lost track of the fact that the punishment that can deter terrorism can also enrage potential terrorists and their supporters; that the prevention of access to targets and resources that can protect targets can also destroy loyalty and alienate those from whom the government needs support; and that monitoring those who are suspects may readily increase the pool of those who must be suspected.

The moral is not that deterrence, restriction of access, and monitoring are not useful steps in preventing terrorism. The message is that even useful steps can have counterproductive sides, and whether the step is, on the whole, helpful or not depends upon assessing that balance. No one is very good at such an assessment, whether the subject is mandatory minimum sentences for drug offenders or dealing with terrorists; but only the foolhardy fail to recognize that the offset is there.

Finally, all this is just part of the problem of prevention of terrorism. Deciding what precisely to do requires more than recognizing trade-offs and competition among the items on a list of what could be done to discourage terrorism. Not every harboring state and not every terrorist group will behave in the same way. The alternatives have to be considered in the far more detailed context of a particular terrorist threat: its leadership, capacities, beliefs, culture, alliances with states and other organizations, and so on. Deciding on a portfolio of actions and a theme to unify and reassure Americans and recruit allies, the final step, depends on also addressing intangible as well as tangible costs. In a very deep way national values will be revealed, and altered, by the choices made in dealing with the dangers of terrorism.

Chapter 4

Intelligence

The obvious limits on the effectiveness of efforts to persuade or deter a sufficiently high percentage of would-be terrorists, and on the prospects for denying anyone who might be a terrorist access to targets and resources, demonstrate the importance of the other major category of state prevention: the gathering and use of intelligence about whom to incapacitate or how to disrupt terrorists' plans.

The Importance of Intelligence

If we know to a sufficient level of certainty that an individual may be planning terrorism, we can disrupt that effort in any of a variety of ways. If our knowledge is adequate and if the plans have proceeded far enough, we can arrest and prosecute for the crimes of conspiracy or attempt to commit the crime. If the evidence is inadequate for this or cannot be revealed, some nations have used detention without prosecution, and we have begun to adopt that practice, even for American citizens. Detention need not be for a crime of terrorism. If the individual suspected of terrorism has violated any other law, such as the conditions of an alien's admission to the United States, we can arrest him on those grounds. If we know who is being relied upon for help, we can disrupt that cooperation. For example, if we know who is providing funds, we can freeze or seize bank accounts or other assets. Individuals who are known to be dangerous can and will be denied access to targets and resources.

We are not restricted to dealing only with the particular individuals intelligence has already identified as currently contemplating or assisting terrorism. The most useful step may be to continue to monitor these individuals until we have identified and then arrested enough of the group to which they belong to deny the group the capacity to carry out any significant form of attack. And if we know who is planning or who has executed a terrorist attack, we can deter that attack or the next one by armed actions against the organization to which the terrorists belong or against any state sponsors. Intelligence plainly expands a state's list of options vastly.

My focus in this chapter is on tactical intelligence, which is intelligence specific enough to allow prevention by incapacitating a critical group of the terrorists or denying them the resources or access their plan requires. That necessitates identifying a sufficient and critical set of participants and learning their plan. But even without meeting these difficult requirements, strategic intelligence—information about an organization's broad motivations and goals, its organizational structure, and its resources and skills—is of great value. For example, strategic intelligence about motivations, even if it does nothing with regard to immediate plans, can provide important clues as to what targets to protect and what methods of attack to fear. If we know about the set of skills and information available to the organization, we will also know far more about what type of threat we have to fear.

Strategic intelligence about organizational structure is also important. If we know whether the organization is more like a governmental or business bureaucracy or, instead, more like a foundation acting on applications from independent parties, we can know much more about the prospects of undercover operations or "working our way up" to the leaders of an organization by making cases at the lowest level and then at the middle level. If we know we are faced with an informal network, we know we have to identify people and needs that are both crucial to coordinated activity and not readily replaced.

That having the wrong organizational structure in mind can be misleading was emphasized by a panel of the National Research Council reporting in 2002:

The preferred organizational form for terrorism is networks or, perhaps better, networks of network-based organizations . . . . As such they are—like other aspects of terrorism—relatively unfamiliar to those who study organizations, who have focused more on formal organizations, such as corporations, hospitals, universities, civil service bureaucracies, voluntary organizations, and organizations developed to direct the activities of social movements. As a result, there are only some, mainly indirect insights about terrorist organizations from the literature on formal organizations.[1]

The intelligence we need—strategic or tactical—can be developed within the United States or abroad. A large terrorist group committed to a campaign of considerable violence against the United States is likely to have long-standing bases outside the country as well as temporary residences within it. Our capacities for gathering intelligence vary, of course, according to whether we are acting within the United States or abroad.

What Went Wrong with Our Intelligence on September 11: The Difficulties of Developing Preventive Intelligence

It is far easier to identify failures of our intelligence on September 11 than to describe what it would take for successful prevention. At the gathering stage, the CIA paid too little attention to the strategic and tactical needs for human intelligence among radical Muslim groups abroad. The FBI paid too little attention to the suspicions and fears of its agents in the field. We were too deferential to the privacy of terrorists connected to religious charities and mosques at home.

The raw information we got—including a strong warning on September 10, 2001—was not translated in a timely fashion. The FBI was computer-challenged. The White House was slow to adopt a strategy for terrorism; one was just bubbling up to the not-so-new president on the day of the attacks. The FBI and the CIA were unwilling or unable to exchange information quickly and effectively; this applied even more to furnishing information to the Immigration and Naturalization Service. The INS did not learn from the CIA what identified terrorists were entering the United States and where they were.

Still more broadly, our attention was diffused. President Clinton had been under attack by those seeking his impeachment.[2] In the area of U.S. relations with the Arab and Muslim worlds, he was seeking a longer-term solution to the conflict between Israel and the Palestinians. We had other items even higher on our agenda with Afghanistan than its harboring of Al Qaeda.

There was a level of complacency, too. We had become accepting of the safe but ineffective response to terrorism represented by our attacks with cruise missiles. We were focused on attacks on Americans abroad, although we should have been able to imagine terrible attacks at home, even of the sort that took place. We had made no adequate effort to protect even the most attractive of targets (the World Trade Center) against attacks with the most available of massive, explosive resources (commercial planes).

The administration has taken steps to remedy many of these failings and others as well. But eliminating many failings whose presence made prevention impossible does not mean that it is now possible to gather the intelligence we need to prevent a future attack.

Gathering enough information for prevention is far more difficult than solving a crime after it has occurred. The latter is a fairly straightforward process. Events leave traces, not only in the form of forensic evidence, such as hair or blood, but also in the memories of the victims, the witnesses, and even the perpetrator (who, for example, may unintentionally provide important clues some days after the crime has occurred). People's personal histories also leave traces. People are seen by friends or business associates. They leave records. An investigation of a crime involves bringing these two sets of traces together. If the investigator has an adequate but small list of suspects—not always an easy accomplishment—she can match the traces of each suspect's personal history with the traces of the crime, looking for similarities too strong to be coincidental. That is what investigation of a past crime is all about.

In the case of prevention, intelligence and law enforcement agencies are looking for traces of a plan, not traces of a completed event. Traces of a plan are more amorphous and more easily hidden, within their own minds, by a small group of conspirators. That difficulty is reflected in the areas where criminal law tries to prevent a planned crime. The proof necessary for the crime of attempt or conspiracy is often more difficult to come by than evidence after the criminal event occurs. Moreover, the shortness of deadlines makes prevention far more difficult. Investigation of a past crime can take years; discovery of a plan for an imminent crime may have to be accomplished in a vastly shorter time. Finally, the demands of completeness are greater for prevention. Solving a past crime by identifying and punishing some of the perpetrators is considered a success; locking up less than a critical mass of a group planning a future crime has to be considered a failure.

There are two ways to develop the intelligence necessary to prevent a terrorist attack. One moves from the early identification of a few suspects to the identification of an indispensable core of participants and their plan. This method is familiar in its broad characteristics but has a considerable capacity for expansion in an information age. The second broad path is from an early detection of a terrorist's plan to identification of a critical core of participants. This path, often called "connecting the dots," poses far more problems. In each case, the intelligence steps can be thwarted by a clever enough opponent.

Developing Intelligence by Moving from a Few Suspects to a Critical Core of Other Participants and an Identification of Their Plan

The most straightforward approach to identification of a critical number of participants and of their plan of attack starts with one or a few previously identified suspects, monitors their activities and associates in a variety of ways, makes sure of a constant readiness to prevent a terrorist attack that may suddenly move toward execution while the gathering of information is continuing, and, finally, arrests and detains the participants.

In this course of activity, the clearest step is moving from one or a few suspects to identification of the larger group or the plan. Physical surveillance (simple observation) can reveal with whom the suspect associates and what his activities are. Phone records of whom he calls and who calls him can be obtained without difficulty from the phone company. With little inconvenience, the government can obtain a variety of records from private organizations, including bank accounts and credit cards, and educational and work records. Many of these records will identify further associates and those receiving or giving financial support. Also, without any requirement of probable cause, the government can use informants to learn secrets from the suspect or to penetrate the group. It can use undercover government employees for the same purpose. If and when the information is strong enough to satisfy the demands of the Fourth Amendment or the Foreign Intelligence Surveillance Act, the government can enter areas of privacy through electronic surveillance or physical searches or arrest followed by interrogation.

Almost all of these devices, except for arrest, can be done covertly, without letting the suspects know they are under surveillance. This is important not only to keep open the opportunity to gather further information about the suspects, but also because, in the case of prevention, very little is gained by arresting or otherwise incapacitating some individuals so long as those participants in the plan who remain undetected still have the capability to carry out the same or a similar mission. Simply knowing the plan allows us to prevent it from taking place at the time and place planned, but that is not enough. The same target can be attacked, or the same resources used, in another place on another occasion, unless significant damage is done to the group. That could require arresting a high percentage of, or those at high levels of, the organization, or using network analysis to determine who is central to its operations and not easily replaced.

The more difficult step is identifying, in the first place, suspects whose activities, if carefully monitored, are likely to reveal other participants and a plan. Three serious problems confront us here. The first is strategic. The terrorist group can make the task of identifying initial suspects considerably more difficult by having much of its plan executed by those with minimal prior contact with those who are already known to be terrorist suspects (and, of course, no prior record of terrorism by the "new faces" themselves). The second is a question of resources. If we conduct surveillance of the sort I have described only on those initial suspects we know to be extremely likely to be engaged in a terrorist plan, we will miss many plans carried out by those we haven't identified as "strong" suspects and their undiscovered associates. But if we engage in extensive surveillance of the contacts of every initial suspect who has any real possibility of being a terrorist, the amount of time and expense involved in carrying out surveillance will be immense. The third problem is that if we focus on monitoring suspects in one group with one plan, overlooking suspects in a separate group with a different plan, whole areas of potential terrorist activities will escape our notice.

Developing an Initial Set of Suspects

How, then, can we take the steps necessary to develop a list of suspects broad enough that, if they are monitored, we are likely to discover the critical mass of participants in each of the terrorist plans we face at any time, but a list still short enough to be manageable?

(1) Forensic evidence from prior terrorist attacks can lead to the discovery of suspects. Those responsible for the bombing of the World Trade Center in 1993 were identified by careful investigation of the crime scene, discovery of a truck identification number, and then the use of records to identify the individual who had rented the truck. Forensic information is generally available only after a terrorist event has taken place and is then useful primarily for attribution of the event to particular individuals who are to be punished, rather than for prevention of the event. But it is a powerful and reliable source of suspects.

(2) Far less reliably, an investigation can develop leads as to initial suspects from neighbors or others who have noticed suspicious activities. That led to identification in the Philippines of Ramsi Yousef, one of the leaders of the World Trade Center bombing of 1993, and himself a terrorist plotting the destruction of a number of airplanes simultaneously over the Pacific. A fire in an apartment raised suspicions (providing us with an example of the rare occasion when an event can be suspicious enough to generate interest even without much of a prior hypothesis). Flight instructors near Minneapolis noticed and reported a set of peculiarities about the behavior of Zacarias Moussaoui, suspected of being "the twentieth hijacker," months before the attacks of September 11.

The neighbors may be motivated by concern about terrorism, their own safety and reputation, or rewards. For the first, it is critical to win and preserve the undivided loyalty (or the unqualified abhorrence of terrorism) of even those to whom the terrorist has most reason to turn for help or for silence. So far, the United States has been blessed—compared with Northern Ireland, Israel, or Italy during the time of the Red Brigades—with a society that does not have deep divisions that the terrorists can exploit or heavily alienated sub-sectors where terrorists can be safe. Terrorists who come to the United States may find safety in anonymity, as those who attacked the World Trade Center did. But we can largely deny terrorists the additional freedom of action and other benefits of sympathy or tolerance. What that takes is competition for the trust, loyalty, and support of the population to whom the terrorist would turn. There is, of course, a trade-off here. Forms of profiling that may be very cheap in terms of inconvenience and dollar cost—such as selective detention of illegal aliens from Muslim countries—may be very expensive in terms of loyalty of neighbors.

Two types of reward have worked to obtain the cooperation of uninvolved associates necessary to identify possible terrorists. Large and well-advertised financial rewards, sometimes accompanied by the protection of being admitted to the United States, have led to revelations about terrorists. After fleeing from the Philippines to Pakistan, Ramsi Yousef was caught by using offers of large rewards on matchbooks. The FBI identified Robert Hanssen, the "mole" within its national security unit, by paying $7 million to a former KGB officer and then relocating him to the United States. Alternatively, in the United States, people arrested know they can reduce their sentence or even obtain immunity by revealing information about far more serious crimes. Terrorism clearly qualifies.

(3) Suspicion may arise and suspects develop from the violent speech of an individual or the enthusiasm of those who are associated with him in political or religious organizations if it is reported by neighbors, informants, or undercover agents. Unlike a number of other countries, the United States does not have a crime of incitement to violence. The Constitution requires an imminent danger or else the type of specific encouragement or aid that would make an individual an accomplice.[3]

The United States does not make membership in organizations committed to violence a crime, and cannot, unless the membership amounts to complicity or conspiracy.[4] Still, terrorist organizations have to recruit from among those who are not already terrorists, and the most likely source of such recruits is those who are members of organizations committed to political violence.

There are serious risks of error in relying for leads on speech, attendance, or membership. Among political organizations, we can often identify those supporting and financing the violence by Palestinians against Israel, but that does not necessarily reveal any intention or willingness to engage in violence against the United States. Even preaching, or cheering, calls for Jihad and the prompt triumph of militant Islam more broadly may be less revealing of any willingness to engage actively in terrorism than of an angry belief that there is a worldwide conspiracy against Muslims, that Israel is a U.S. wedge to prevent unity of the Muslim world, and that bringing Muslim religious law to governments of the Middle East and elsewhere would be glorious.

The number of false positives if one were using just these criteria as evidence of active terrorism would be great. Other statements and beliefs would have to differentiate those likely to be violent—beliefs such as that an Islamic order should rule the entire world, that non-Muslims can and should be killed, and that Muslim regimes which are "illegitimate" should be overthrown. These are distinctions that are likely to be hidden in ambiguous language and prove too subtle for us to expect an agent attending a mosque to make at the peril of dividing the society along religious lines.

(4) Sometimes suspects can be found by countersurveillance of people apparently "casing" a target area.

(5) Finally, Germany has learned to search for suspects by detailed analysis of patterns of otherwise mundane data. In the years of the Red Army Faction, unusual electricity bills were useful in identifying "safe houses." Relatively rare combina-

tions of demographic and economic data are now used by Germany in an effort to identify possible members of terrorist groups after September 11.[5] Indeed, Section 98A of the German Criminal Procedure Code specifically authorizes that, in national security cases:

... [P]ersonal data ... relating to certain presumed characteristics of the perpetrator may be compared by machine with other data in order to exclude other individuals under suspicion, or to identify individuals who meet other characteristics significant to the investigations.

A closely related effort directed at airline security by our Transportation Security Administration was described by Robert O'Harrow in the *Washington Post*:

Under the plan, passengers would be required, when making their reservations, to provide identifying information, such as a name, address, and driver's license, passport, Social Security and frequent-flier numbers. Those details would be used by private data services, such as ChoicePoint, Inc., an identification and verification company, to supply more information about the individual.

TSA computers would then use artificial intelligence and other sophisticated software, along with behavior models developed by intelligence agencies, to determine whether the passenger is "rooted in the community"—whether he or she is well established in the United States—and find links to others who might be terrorists, according to government documents and interviews.

The aim is to create an "automated system capable of integrating and simultaneously analyzing numerous databases from Government, industry and the private sector ... which establishes a threat risk assessment on every air carrier passenger, airport and flight," according to a government document.[6]

Preventive Intelligence: Moving from Discovery of a Likely Plan to Identification of Suspects

Without intelligence or suspicion of a plan, we can attempt to protect certain targets and to deny certain resources to anyone who might threaten them. As described in the last chapter, access to particular locations can be denied to anyone who has not received a careful vetting and subsequent clearance. The locations can be picked as those which are most important to us or, where this differs, which would be the most attractive targets to likely terrorists. Resources could be chosen because of the danger they pose and the feasibility of denying access to them or because of their attractiveness to terrorists, perhaps based on their capacity to create panic (e.g., a "dirty" but conventional bomb laced with radioactive materials).

For many reasons this approach is inadequate. There are far too many attractive targets in the United States and far too many ways to attack them. Moreover, the terrorists have the advantage of "second move"—focusing their attacks on what has not already been protected. We can try to keep our steps of protection secret and try to outguess the attackers, using such devices as "Red" attack teams trying to outsmart "Blue" protective teams. Still, the advantage remains heavily with the terrorist attacker.

Not much is added by a somewhat random effort to spot patterns and connect the dots among a large number of events being monitored. Only the patterns that one already suspects, at least unconsciously, are detected by looking at a mass of information. Without knowing what targets to fear for, or what resources to fear, it is difficult to know where to look—which collection of events and other facts to scan.

If critical "dots" are not part of public records, we would need sizeable numbers of informed people to look for them in the mass of everyday life. If they are held in private places, we need authority to go there. Even when suspicious dots are found, despite all this, we have to be able to separate innocent forms of activity from dangerous forms. The difficulty is clear enough. I hardly need add the problems of bringing together observations and insights from a number of different agencies.

What can be done? First, we can look for suspicious combinations of information, hoping they will produce a greatly

a. addition

b. subtraction

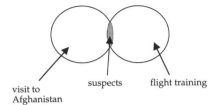

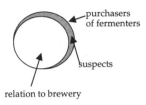

Figure 4.1 Developing Suspects from Computerized Matching of Fields of Data

reduced field of suspects. The combination may take the form of an addition. All those seeking flight training who have spent more than three weeks in Afghanistan might warrant being treated as suspects. The combination might instead be a subtraction. Someone buying fermenting equipment who has no contact with a brewery might be treated as a suspect in terms of the dangers of anthrax. Both methods are often called "data mining." The technique has been used extensively to discover false welfare claims among those on the federal payroll or other unlikely and suspicious combinations of two innocent fields of data. In diagram form, the small number of suspects could be idealized in either of the ways shown in Figure 4.1.

More complex combinations of factors might be necessary to reduce the list of suspects to an even more manageable level. There might be other legitimate uses for fermenters, and a failure to identify those other uses will leave too large a list of unimportant suspects. On the other hand, a person visiting Afghanistan may be hard to identify as a suspect since one could easily fly into a neighboring country and then drive. Instead, we might look for persons who have flight training and have visited two or more countries on a specific list within the past three years.

The data need not be from prior records. With information far less substantial than that required to deny someone access to a person, place, or location, we would be justified in keeping a list of those who could be exploring targets or resources. Matching this list with either a list of those who have sought access to dangerous substances or those whose activities have suggested terrorist training would create a very useful list of suspects.

For some targets that seem to us particularly likely to be attacked and some resources that seem to us particularly likely to be used, we could develop likely terrorist scenarios and lists of indicators that one of those scenarios is being acted upon by a previously unidentified group. If information available without costly investigative steps was being used, the capacity of computers might allow us to monitor hundreds of those scenarios. When enough of those indicators had appeared to suggest that there was a significant (perhaps 5 to 10 percent) chance that a terrorist plan was underway, we could move to investigative techniques focused on those already identified and the scenario their activities suggest. In particularly sensitive areas, such as attending aviation school or studying nuclear science, we could monitor for any significant departures from the normal, much as we have monitored doctors' billing of Medicare for such "outliers."

Once again, it is important to remember that intelligence is a game of strategy played by competitors. Each of these devices for moving from discovery of a plan to discovery of its participants, or to discovery of suspects whose associates and activities can then be monitored, can be avoided, defeated, or misdirected. It is as important to the terrorist to learn our ways of detecting his activity as it is to us to detect what he is doing. High measures of secrecy may be required on our side, as they are on the terrorists'. Sometimes our secrecy can be penetrated, and the value of our screening system sharply undermined, by surprisingly simple stratagems.[7]

Moving from Suspicion Generated in Either of These Ways to Preventive Action

The steps from intelligence to prevention depend on what form of action is called upon. Different forms of preventive action require establishing different levels of certainty to different fact-finders.

Commitment to a prison (as in the case of those responsible for the first World Trade Center bombing or the African embassy bombings) requires conviction of a crime, which in turn requires proof beyond a reasonable doubt. Deportation requires something less, but still clear and convincing evidence. Detention pending trial for a crime or for an immigration violation requires only "probable cause," as does the seizure of assets. And detention and conviction or deportation intended to disable a terrorist can be for an unrelated minor crime or for an immigration violation.

President Bush has claimed the administrative power to detain citizens or aliens who may be illegal combatants without specifying the government's burden of proof.[8] The slightest of suspicions can be used to shift the travel plans of whoever might be attacked, or used to add weight to the other evidence in a file at home or abroad. It can also be used to precipitate additional investigative steps that do not require demonstrating probable cause of a crime or that someone is a foreign agent.

These last matters are decided by the investigators alone. Similarly, the basis for the president's judgment that someone should be detained is not, under his directives, reviewable by any even quasi-independent fact finder,[9] although the courts may require some review. Immigration matters go to administrative judges, but the attorney general can often insist on detention pending deportation. The basis for asset forfeiture must be shown to a judge, and the same is true for conviction of any crime, unless the courts sustain the president's claim of a right to use military tribunals for aliens, even those living in the United States, suspected of some involvement with international terrorism.

In sum, the balance at this third stage between further investigative effort and preventive action against suspects or their assets depends not only on investigative strategy but also on how much the law requires to be proven and to whose satisfaction. The government can often choose among ways of accomplishing detention when the purpose is incapacitation of a dangerous suspect or interrogation of one who may have useful information. It can "move the goal posts" formally by establishing forms of detention whose requirements (or decision-makers) are more easily satisfied. It can do much the same informally by arresting for violations of law that are generally ignored.

To meet even a reduced burden of proof, let alone a requirement like "probable cause of criminal conduct," the initial leads are not likely to be sufficient. The government must build on them. An intermediate level of proof short of that needed for some of the preventive steps may allow the use in the United States of intrusive investigative techniques such as electronic and physical searches. If the initial leads (even when they are combined with others) do not meet that intermediate level, the government can often reach it—if its suspicions are true—by greatly increasing its number of investigators. They can search for and analyze publicly available or freely provided information or documents; and they can freely use interviews, informants, undercover agents, or physical surveillance (all of which are available without any showing of evidence of likely guilt). The government has made it easier to reach that intermediate level needed for more intrusive searches in the United States by somewhat lowering the standard in the case of agents of a foreign state or group engaged in terrorism.[10] And none of the barriers to intrusive physical or electronic searches apply abroad unless an American citizen or resident is targeted.

Finally, in any of these ways as well as in any number of ways that are illegal for U.S. agents, foreign intelligence or law enforcement agencies may have discovered and then furnished us information adequate either for one of the forms of prevention in the United States or to authorize a search or electronic surveillance here.

Prospects for Intelligence-Gathering Abroad

The small operational cells adequate for the attacks by Al Qaeda were able to survive in the United States for some years prior to September 11. It is very difficult for a law enforcement or internal security agency to detect the activities of small numbers of cautious people, even if they are illegally within the United States. But to mount a sustained terrorist campaign against the United States, more than four or five or even 20 individuals are necessary. There has to be a relatively sizeable ongoing organization to raise money, recruit and train volunteers, establish contacts for help with resources and skills, choose targets for maximum impact, and so on.

The mass of the organization, Al Qaeda, was detectable and its general location—based in Afghanistan—was easily discoverable. A critical requirement for terrorists to mount a sustained campaign from abroad against the United States is that they be able to build and maintain for sustained periods a significant organization abroad, despite the efforts of law enforcement and internal security agencies in the states where the organization is located.

That capacity may depend upon the host state's tolerance of the organization's activities, as in the case of Afghanistan. For example, many of the steps necessary for recruiting terrorists may be easily discovered by internal security agents of a somewhat despotic host government *if* it wants to stop the terror. To recruit to any sizeable organization requires at least minimal forms of advertising, and this exposes the organization to informants. Training and indoctrination in anger and hatred require schools or other meeting places that can be discovered and monitored. Charismatic leadership requires public exposure. What is likely beyond U.S. reach—recruitment and training abroad—can be greatly curbed with the help of the host country.

To prevent the terrorist organization from operating, the host state would have to aggressively use its domestic intelligence and law enforcement capacities to find and punish the terrorists. The more undemocratic, the more despotic the state, the more likely it will have in place the capacities for the job, because intelligence agents will already have been trained to protect the undemocratic government against its challengers. Fortunately, it is in such despotic states that Al Qaeda finds most of its supporters and its havens. Unfortunately, in such states despotism, corruption, and dependence on the United States often generate substantial and threatening dissident movements; and support by these governments for our efforts to counter terrorism increases the hatred and opposition of the dissidents, both toward the United States, which is already resented for its influence over the local government, and for the government, much of whose population may share many of the terrorists' grievances.

We need cooperation. The crucial tasks of gathering intelligence abroad are *not* ones the United States can carry out by itself. Demands for access for investigators or even military forces to help conduct law enforcement operations in states like Syria, Libya, or Sudan will be resisted as requiring too significant a sacrifice of sovereignty. As noted previously, Saudi Arabia would not give the FBI a free hand to investigate the 1996 bombing of the Khobar Towers. Even if allowed, moreover, U.S. agents are not likely to find terrorists in an unfriendly setting, without taking over the country and mounting a costly and repressive occupation.

The United States may be able to locate and capture terrorist leaders abroad, but it will remain difficult to prove personal guilt beyond a reasonable doubt. For this reason we abandoned efforts a decade ago to extradite the Palestine Liberation Front leader, Abu Abbas, for the seizure of the *Achille Lauro* and, in 1996, declined to take custody of Osama Bin Laden despite his terrorist efforts before that date.[11] For that reason, President

Bush created military tribunals with more sympathetic fact-finders and eased rules of evidence. The alternative of assassinating a terrorist leader abroad may create in the terrorist group a vacuum of leadership, or demoralization, or a harmful conflict over new leadership.[12] But it also threatens retaliatory efforts (such as Israel has repeatedly experienced), the recruitment benefits to the terrorists of martyrdom, and the profound embarrassment of occasionally killing innocent people. Because it gives grave offense to the sovereignty of a state where we kill an individual, assassination as a policy instrument can be used only in hostile states or with the consent of a friendly state; and, in the latter case, only in the absence of the state's capacity to effect an arrest. And, with these drawbacks, assassination creates a precedent that precludes our denouncing others and makes the world a far more dangerous place for our leaders, too.

THE LIMITS OF OUR CAPACITY TO ELICIT THE COOPERATION OF FOREIGN INTELLIGENCE AGENCIES

The United States will have to rely on the efforts of the law enforcement and internal security forces of states where the terrorist organizations are operating. As I have argued in Chapter 2, threats alone will be inadequate to create reliable cooperation. Some states will lack the competence to really help, and other states that do not believe in the cause will make efforts too half-hearted to be effective but real enough to be indistinguishable from sanctionable incompetence. And there is little the United States will be able to do when a state where terrorists may be planning attacks plausibly claims it cannot find them. Greece's leading terrorist organization operated in Greece against U.S. officials for decades before the first arrests were made by the Greek government in 2002.[13]

In sum, all that the United States can accomplish by the threat of military force or other sanctions is to end state support or tolerance of terrorism where it is now open or where it is likely to be discovered. That will not prevent secret support or tolerance. Better concealment is always a possible response to a threat of punishment. Such concealed support can continue at least as long as the host state can pretend to be unable to locate, let alone control, the terrorist organization. For, in the absence of proof of bad faith, any U.S. military response will threaten the continued support of coalition partners and cause widespread suspicion of injustice within the United States and abroad.

With feigned good faith an effective reply to military threats, the best bet—one that the U.S. government is presently pursuing—is a combination of military threat, economic or political inducements, and a moral campaign against terrorism. To win the sincere cooperation of the internal security and law enforcement forces of the states where terrorist organizations are located, the United States will have to form mutually beneficial alliances as well as make a persuasive ideological case against terrorism wherever it takes place and whomever it targets, not just terrorism targeted against the United States. The former will require rewards as well as threats. The latter will require abandoning U.S. support or even sympathy for groups that are attacking civilians in any country whose enthusiastic support the United States wants in tracking down terrorist organizations. The case will have to be made that no one's terrorists are "freedom fighters."

Even if the United States can coax or coerce the full support of a state where an organization such as Al Qaeda is located, that may not end the threat. I have noted in Chapter 2 that terrorist organizations whose support by one state has been withdrawn may find alternative support in another state that is unrelentingly hostile to the United States and prepared to bear the consequences. And the terrorist organization may be able to operate despite good faith efforts to eliminate it by the state where it is located. After all, even the British could not disable the IRA during its most dangerous years, and U.S. authorities took seven years to apprehend Eric Rudolph, suspected in the bombing at the Atlanta Olympics. Like organized crime, a terrorist group may be able to survive the most steely of state opposition.

THE MORAL, LEGAL, AND LEADERSHIP COSTS OF RELIANCE ON THE UNLIMITED POWERS OF INTELLIGENCE AGENCIES OF DESPOTIC GOVERNMENTS

The Charter of the United Nations and the Geneva Conventions with their protocols limit the occasions in which a nation may make war, define the protection a state must give civilian populations, and specify treatment to which captured enemy forces are entitled. The applicability of these rules to terrorism, their requirements, and especially the question of the extent to which we are responsible for the behavior of forces we support or have empowered are obviously matters of major importance.[14]

Not addressed, although equally important, is a fundamental choice we will face for years between our safety and the human rights of citizens of other nations. In fact, we can reduce the danger to Americans at the cost of reducing the liberties and rights of others. There are potentially effective measures for other nations to gather information that, while helpful in prevention or punishment, we would regard as improper to apply to U.S. citizens and to others in the United States. Torture is an obvious example. These methods are also inconsistent with the image of a decent, or even benevolent, United States— an image that is a valuable asset in garnering support against terrorism. Encouraging their use in some instances also denies us the power to complain about their broader use by others.

We have, and hopefully will maintain, careful limits on interrogation, protective requirements for searches or electronic surveillance, and strong public resistance to the Bush administration's exercise of its claim of power to seize an individual without probable cause and detain him indefinitely. Torture will not comfortably return to the United States. But these protections are often not available in anything like the same measure in a state where terrorists are likely to seek haven. That country's internal security structure and police apparatus is likely to be far less constrained if activated by the CIA on our behalf.

The United States can reap the immediate benefits of these activities, forbidden by international human rights conventions, when the activities are directed at an individual abroad planning terrorism against the United States. And investigation at that stage, where a terrorist group is likely to be operating the facilities necessary for recruiting, training, and financing attacks on the United States, is also likely to look more promising than discovering small cells temporarily based in the United States.

Thus the most serious questions of human rights, and of the price we are prepared to pay in terms of lost respect for the United States, will arise not here but abroad if we attempt to export the human counterterrorism costs of extensive searches, electronic surveillance, coercive interrogation, detention, and limitations on association and speech. Each of these measures, controlled or forbidden at home by the U.S. Constitution and abroad by international conventions, are likely to be promising ways of getting needed information about terrorists' plans and of otherwise preventing terrorist planning. But each can prove extremely costly in the longer run.

Our moral and legal responsibility for violations of human rights that are intended, at least in significant part, to protect us depends upon two issues. First, what forms of inquiry by U.S. officials become requests for actions by other states in violation of conventions to which we have adhered? Second, to what extent does U.S. encouragement become irrelevant when it is likely that the human rights, perhaps of the same people, would be ignored by the state where they reside anyway?

There is a continuum of U.S. actions relevant to these questions. At one extreme, hoping to elicit information about the terrorist events, we could threaten—as we did with a suspect in the bombing of the Khobar Towers barracks in Saudi Arabia—to send suspects who are in our hands to another country where they will be treated far less carefully. Or we could send them abroad for interrogation as we did with a German sent to Syria.[15] At the other extreme would be actions by a nation friendly to the United States which were not motivated by a desire to protect the United States. In between there are any number of foreseeable violations of "protected" human rights by foreign police and intelligence agencies, including many in which the CIA will know of the capture of individuals and may make known to the international security apparatus of a foreign nation exactly what it would like to know.

Conclusion

Both the needed processes and the objectives of intelligence-gathering are clear. To prevent a terrorist event (and any immediate substitute for it) intelligence must identify a critical number of the group involved and do that secretly so they can be found and incapacitated. Just to prevent a particular terrorist event—leaving ourselves exposed to a prompt substitute—intelligence must discover the planned target or needed resources. The process needed to accomplish one of these objectives can start with some suspects or, with greater difficulty, with early suspicions of a particular plan. How to move creatively from either starting point is also moderately clear.

Any great hope of using intelligence to prevent terrorism must rely on freely given cooperation of foreign governments and the work of their law enforcement and intelligence agencies. We cannot effectively police the level of investigative activity that will be necessary. Even freely given cooperation will be costly, economically in terms of what we will have to pay, politically in terms of reciprocal support against those challenging the government supporting us, and morally in terms of what we accept as legitimate methods of extracting information.

Part III

Recognizing the Costs of the Steps We Take

Chapter 5

Civil Liberties

A concise way of stating the argument so far is this: Nothing dictates or requires the use of the metaphor of war to suggest and justify the steps we should take after September 11. Whether we use that metaphor or the less accessible but more revealing division of terrorism into almost a dozen categories of threat, several of which are new to us, is a matter of pragmatic choice. In the final analysis, what we should be doing is reviewing, skeptically, what is on our menu of choices and then choosing not what is popular but what is most likely to be effective in protecting our security in the short run and in the long run. The metaphor of war makes this more difficult. It tends to obscure the differences among the threats we face and to distract attention from a careful analysis of: what we can do; what the essential roles of other nations are; and what mixture of desired and undesired effects is likely for each of our choices.

An Overview

This picture still leaves out one critically important dimension of choice. Even what is effective in protecting the safety of American citizens and their property may be unwise because of its effects on the historic set of arrangements which have preserved our democratic liberties. A more complete picture of what bears on our choices can be captured in a simple diagram, Figure 5.1.

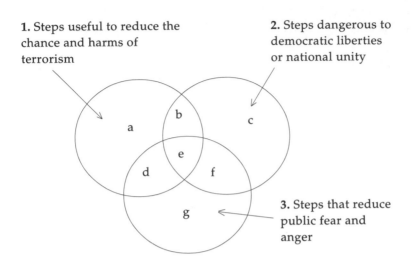

1. Steps useful to reduce the chance and harms of terrorism

2. Steps dangerous to democratic liberties or national unity

3. Steps that reduce public fear and anger

Figure 5.1 Choice of Actions Incorporating Democratic Freedoms and Political Demands as well as Efficacy

The content of circles 1 and 3—steps effective in dealing with terrorism and steps effective in dealing with public anger and fear—is clear enough. But what I am adding here is the content of circle 2, steps that cause harm to democratic liberties or undermine national unity. Characteristically, the harms take two distinct forms: abandoning those constraints on executive action that are necessary to a feeling of public confidence that one is not threatened by his own government; and a focusing on one group within the population for far more than ordinary levels of suspicion and caution because its members share religion, ethnicity, or racial background with the terrorists.

The small letters in the diagram reflect the mixture of hard and easy choices that must be made. The steps marked "a" and "d" should obviously be taken unless they are too costly in terms of resources. Steps in the area marked "c" are ones that no one ought to take, and no one would want to. Wisdom and courage are required in the other areas. Courageous leaders will hesitate to take steps marked in the popularly demanded area "f," although they may take relatively useless measures in the area "g." The hardest decisions, requiring the most wisdom, are those in areas "b" and "e."

Consider carefully area "f": steps that are not helpful in reducing the danger, are harmful to democratic liberties, and are tempting because they are popular. What makes matters dangerous to democratic liberties turns out to be straightforward. What keeps even popular actions that reduce public fear and express public anger from being persuasive as sensible efforts to reduce the chance and harm of terrorism is that they are not plausibly related to a reduction in terrorist motivations or capacities. For example, they may fail the simple evaluative process described in Chapter 8. Alternatively, they may be too plausibly related to political advantage or administrative convenience. These characteristics were, for example, the focus of the condemnation by the American Bar Association's Coordinating Committee on Immigration Law of "the incommunicado detention of immigrants in undisclosed locations . . ."[1] The need to abandon the safeguards of transparency was barely explained, and was not reviewed by coordinate branches. Moreover, the need for this form of detention could not survive probing analysis.

There is only one real justification for knowingly moving into area "f" on the chart. My focus has been on steps designed to prevent terrorism. Minimizing the consequences of a terrorist event, while outside the scope of this book, is also of immense importance. Generally, we think of consequence management as organizing, equipping, and training those who must respond to a massive attack in such a way as to make the responses as prompt and effective as possible. The focus is on medical personnel, firefighters, police, and specialists in emergency situations. Nations have, however, responded to terrorist attacks with retaliation in situations where deterrence was extremely unlikely.[2] Israel is a leading example, but the United States, with our cruise missile attacks during the 1990s in Iraq, Afghanistan and Sudan, provides additional examples. What the attacks do accomplish is to support the morale of a population that has been injured and feels vulnerable to further injury. In this, the motivation is like the demand for retribution in criminal law. Retaliation, in short, is often a form of consequence management where the consequence being managed is the morale of the population that has been attacked. Steps taken in the "f" area may be defensible as consequence management, even when they are not justifiable as danger preventing.

When there is a true conflict between greater security and preserving historic democratic freedoms (as in areas "b" and "e"), we must do our best to choose wisely—not an easy assignment in times of danger and fear. Still, it must be done. Some would argue that the choice should be made, on balance, without any presumption in favor of a particular result; others, that a presumption of holding firm to what has served us well for many decades should tilt the scale toward preserving democratic freedoms unless the case for substantially increased security is quite clear. What isn't permissible is the view that Attorney General Ashcroft has repeatedly enunciated: that the job of the Justice Department is to go as far as legally possible in protecting even limited amounts of security without consideration of the long-term costs in democratic freedoms; i.e, that *every* legal action falling into in areas "b" and "e" should be done.

It may not be entirely fair to say that the Bush administration has taken the position that it has no responsibility to weigh the costs in democratic freedoms of steps that have even a limited prospect of providing us with more physical safety; for the administration of course recognizes that it should not, can not, and will not violate clear law. What it has sought to do is to ignore the responsibility of the executive to consider the impact of precedent and practice on the character of the country and to deny the Congress and the courts the opportunity to exercise oversight. Furthermore, it has sought to deny the American people full knowledge of what is being done.[3]

The Impact on Democratic Freedoms of Three Questionable Themes of the Bush Administration's Domestic Strategy of Counterterrorism

1. REDUCTION OF BURDENS OF PROOF AND ABANDONMENT OF THE NECESSITY OF PRESENTING PUBLIC EVIDENCE BEFORE DETENTION

One major step the administration has taken to protect the United States against terrorism is to find ways to detain individuals where there is a real possibility of involvement with terrorism but the probability is relatively low. In this category it has been particularly inventive. The president's "military order" permits the secretary of defense to direct indefinite detention of any alien, including resident aliens, who has been found to support international terrorism of any sort.[4] Without an amended presidential order, the president and the secretary of defense extended the detention power to U.S. citizens, even if arrested in the United States and far from any battlefield.[5]

Quite simply, a country cannot be free if the Executive retains the power, on its own determination that certain conditions are met, to detain citizens for an indefinite period. In both the case of citizens and the case of aliens there was an explicit effort to deny judicial review of the crucial findings on the basis of which it was claimed that the individual could be detained indefinitely.[6]

These awesome and threatening claims of executive power have hardly been used because the administration has been able to detain more than 1,200 aliens for significant periods of time by manipulation of arrest, detention, and removal practices with regard to aliens guilty of unauthorized stays within the United States or by a nearly unprecedented use of the statute allowing detention of witnesses who otherwise may not be available to testify. It has carefully exploited the right to use selective enforcement of rarely used statutes and powers to act against a group or an activity for purposes largely unconnected with the purposes of the Congress in passing the statute.

In developing a strategy for use of its powers for purposes for which the powers were never intended, the administration has gone well beyond the carefully targeted use of the power to arrest. In the case of immigration laws, it has also used its right to control many enforcement choices to delay filing charges, delay hearings, and delay deportation orders after decision.[7] All of this discretion was given because of the administrative needs of enforcing the immigration laws. There are about 20 million aliens in the United States at any given time, a high percentage of whom are at least technically in violation of one or another visa regulation. But that fact is now being used as a device for holding suspects—most only weakly linked to terrorism—for purposes of interrogation or incapacitation.

This technique is also behind a quite novel application of the government's power to detain citizens and non-citizens as material witnesses so as to include, in addition to the relatively narrow class of trial witnesses, the open-ended category of prospective witnesses before an investigating grand jury. Under this interpretation, any of us, citizens included, could be detained as a material witness before a grand jury—an institution largely controlled by prosecutors that has wide scope to investigate without serious judicial review.

The administration has made no serious effort to argue that detention rather than arrest would be necessary in the case of any individual as to whom there was probable cause of involvement in even the early stages of planning for international terrorism. In fact, the administration does not claim solid information as to terrorism about more than a very small percentage of those who have been detained. The purpose of the detention powers is to reach those who might be terrorists but might not be proved to be terrorists. Subjecting this vastly larger class to detention makes a fundamental change in the relation of American citizens, resident aliens, and visitors to those governing the United States. The change has been made without serious explanation. Even with an explanation, any such change should be made by legislation, not by the Executive. It has been tolerable to Americans only because it is implicitly and seemingly reliably limited to discrete groups to which most do not belong.

2. CRIMINAL PUNISHMENT WITHOUT CRIMINAL STATUTES, JUDGES, OR JURIES

Changes in the level of proof necessary to detain individuals are closely related to efforts to try those individuals under less onerous rules of evidence, before a more readily persuadable tribunal. In a military order, the president has in fact claimed the right to try, convict, and sentence non-citizens living in the United States who may be connected to international terrorism without the open display of evidence that our courts and constitution generally require.[8] The trial would be before a military tribunal made up of officers who report to the secretary of defense, not before a judge and jury; and the proceedings need not be public. The proof need not satisfy traditional rules of evidence, so long as "a reasonable person" would consider it to have "probative value." The identity of witnesses may be hidden, as in Colombia or Peru. Convictions would not require a unanimous vote. There is to be no civilian judicial review of a conviction.

None of this has been authorized by Congress; no evidence that it is necessary has been offered. The United States has criminal statutes that apply to terrorists attacking Americans abroad. Additionally, the Classified Information Procedures Act[9] allows the use of classified materials without unnecessarily compromising secrets. The United States has a witness protection program to protect endangered witnesses and a variety of devices to protect jurors. We have, and have exercised, the capacity to bring terrorists back from the other side of the world for trial in the United States.[10] With this array of legal and political powers, the United States has been able to prosecute the terrorists responsible for bombing the World

Trade Center and our embassies in Kenya and Tanzania, spies for the Soviet Union such as Aldrich Ames, Mafia chieftains like John Gotti, and drug lords such as Manuel Noriega.

Prosecuting dangerous terrorists in United States courts presents no difficulties distinct from these other high-profile areas. It is gathering convincing evidence against those sponsoring terrorism that has proven difficult. In the trial of two Libyans for blowing up Pan Am Flight 103 over Lockerbie, one accused was acquitted and no charges were brought against superiors up to Moammar Khadafy, although those tried for the terrorist explosion were believed to be acting for Libya. Lacking evidence, the United States withdrew its request for arrest and extradition of Abu Abbas for leading the hijackers of the *Achille Lauro*. Despite major investigative efforts, it remains unclear who directed the bombing in Saudi Arabia of the U.S. military housing at Khobar Towers. But conviction without strong evidence is not defensible.

Still, on November 13, 2001, President Bush signed a military order allowing the trial, in military courts with penalties up to death, of any individual who is not a U.S. citizen (including 20 million within the United States) for activities, even within the United States, that the president determines involve international terrorism or harboring international terrorists.[11] Administrative and operational considerations may support the use of military tribunals for those captured on a battlefield and charged with violations of the laws of war. But only a desire to convict with less or different evidence explains a claim to use such tribunals when civilian law and courts are readily available and the defendant was found within the United States.[12]

The British "Diplock Courts" for Northern Ireland are perhaps the most famous of the special anti-terrorism courts in operation. Although they were a far less serious departure from normal criminal trial procedures than the Bush administration's initiatives, these modified courts, lacking normal jury and other protections, still became a *cause célèbre* in

Northern Ireland and generated substantial sympathy for the terrorist cause.[13] Military trials in the United States based on an unreviewed suspicion of unidentified forms of support of undefined political violence with an unspecific international connection will similarly undermine the support and loyalty of many millions here in the United States and their relatives abroad.[14] At the same time, they will stifle speech and legitimate dissent among those covered.

The military order deprives the United States of its historic claim of moral leadership among the world's nations in matters of fairness to individuals charged with crime, leaving us in the company of dictators like President Robert Mugabe of Zimbabwe.[15] It makes even more difficult future efforts at military coalition-building and will deny us the benefits of legal cooperation with our closest allies in the forms of extradition and mutual legal assistance.[16] Finally, it will leave lasting doubts about the honesty of convictions in the wake of secret trials with secret evidence.[17]

3. AVOIDING JUDICIAL, LEGISLATIVE, OR VOTER PARTICIPATION IN DECISIONS REGARDING COUNTERTERRORISM

The president's military order and the decision, adding to that order, to detain indefinitely an American citizen, Jose Padilla, arrested within the United States[18] are accompanied by the specification that there should be no significant judicial review of the detention. The same is true, of course, for enemy combatants held at the U.S. base at Guantanamo Bay, Cuba, and claiming the rights of prisoners of war. The same is true of anyone held by use of the immigration laws. In addition, amendments to the immigration statute, at the administration's request, have denied review by administrative judges of decisions denying release on bail.[19]

The contrast with Israel is revealing. Even in the midst of the intifada, the Israeli Supreme Court has asserted some level of

judicial review over government actions that affect Palestinians, both within Israel and also within the West Bank and
Gaza. Not only has the Israeli Supreme Court banned the use
of torture in interrogations,[20] it has also insisted that administrative detentions and house demolitions be reviewed by the
courts, even though this review is at times conducted through
the military court system.[21] In stark contrast, the Bush administration has argued, with some success, that there is no judicial
review at all of the detention and treatment of those non-
citizens held outside the United States at Guantanamo,[22] and
that the most minimal form of judicial review is available to an
American citizen detained and questioned without a lawyer
and without access to family for an indefinite period.[23] There
would be no or next-to-no judicial review of the propriety of
the determination that an alien is subject to trial as a terrorist
before a military tribunal.[24]

The view of the Bush administration has been consistent:
that the location at which a non-citizen is held, the battlefield
conditions under which he was seized, the absence of uniform,
or a threat to willingly cause civilian deaths will preclude any
significant form of judicial review for almost anyone whom the
administration suspects of involvement with terrorists. Though
our danger is far less than the danger that Israel faces, our
willingness to abandon the most fundamental judicial protections of personal security has been far greater.

A strategy that directs administration officials to go as far as
law will allow, without any executive responsibility to consider democratic freedoms, has *no* limits if there is to be no
judicial review of what the law allows. Determinations by the
administration are not adequate in that regard. In addition, the
administration has gone out of its way to deny access to
lawyers for most of the grounds it relies on for detention.
Where denial has been impossible, nothing has been done to
facilitate the access of lawyers to those secretly detained.

Nor have the checks implicit in maintaining a separation of
executive, judicial, and legislative powers been accomplished by

a congressional role. The detentions are not, in most cases, on grounds that Congress has authorized. The judiciary committees were long denied oversight of new powers granted by the USA Patriot Act.[25] The intelligence committees, to which alone the administration acknowledges the duty to report, have complained that they are not granted adequate information.[26]

Whatever check on executive powers the voting public might impose depends upon the public knowing what the Executive is doing. In the name of protection against discovery of our secrets by terrorist enemies, the administration has denied almost any obligation of transparency.

Adam Clymer of the *New York Times* summarized the situation with regard to secrecy in early 2003, saying: "The Bush administration has put a much tighter lid than recent presidents on government proceedings and the public release of information, exhibiting a penchant for secrecy that has been striking historians, legal experts, and law makers of both parties." Clymer quotes Columbia historian Alan Brinkley as saying that "while secrecy has been increasingly attractive to recent administrations, 'this administration has taken it to a new level.'" He quotes Senator Patrick Lahey as saying that in the 29 years he has been in Congress, "I've never known an administration that is more difficult to get information from."[27] There are always two effects of governmental secrecy about matters of domestic security: both our enemies and our citizens are kept in the dark, and sometimes the latter is much of the purpose.

Courts have now ordered some accounting of those few still being detained for a variety of reasons without judicial review, arguing that a democracy cannot tolerate the knowledge that the administration, for reasons that it will not explain, has detained in places it will not state well over 1,200 people it will not name (the exact number has been kept secret).[28] Other courts have ordered that deportation hearings cannot be kept secret from family and press on the mere say-so of the administration and without giving reasons to the courts.[29] Access to "illegal combatants" in Guantanamo is severely limited. The intelligence committees have been restricted in what they can make public, even when the matter appears to be of greater political than national security importance (such as what the administration was told about the dangers of attack before September 11).[30]

Three Unavoidable Choices Impacting Democratic Freedoms and Unity

Decisions that fall into areas "b" and "e" in Figure 5.1 pose unavoidable and difficult decisions about whether the security justification for a step is adequate in light of its harmful impact on democratic freedoms. For those who believe there should be a presumption against departing from long traditions protective of individuals against a powerful executive, any uncertainty should be resolved in favor of traditional liberties. Even for those who would simply weigh costs against benefits, without any presumption, the issues are close and the answers debatable. What is not debatable is that these decisions should be made by the Congress, as well as the president, after careful consideration of the costs to our freedoms. In the case of the USA Patriot Act, the Congress has participated, but in many cases it has not. Nor in the cases I am about to discuss is there any indication that the executive branch has itself given serious consideration to the price of its proposals in terms of democratic liberties.

1. WHETHER TO CONCENTRATE INVESTIGATIVE RESOURCES ON NATIONALS OF ARAB OR MUSLIM STATES

Serious problems for civil liberties and equal protection emerge from profiling proposals. Measures that generalize about danger on the basis of nationality, religion, or ethnic classification range from the "enemy alien" detentions of Germans, Italians, and Japanese during World War II, to denying entire national, ethnic, or religious categories access to targets or resources, to taking the investigative steps to develop more information about members of any of these groups. Yet the case for some such measures in terms of effectiveness in producing increased security (i.e., omitting for the moment the costs in terms of civil liberties and foreign relations) in fighting terrorism could be strong.

Whether placing some reliance on these factors is effective in increasing security depends on considering both how it helps produce security and how it hurts the same effort. A sensible policy would not ignore several ways such selectivity could hurt our security. It may hurt by misdirecting our attention and energies away from more reliable indicators of danger, for example, recent travel to Afghanistan, or from more reliable processes of intelligence-gathering (such as the pursuit of contacts of a known terrorist). Or it may dangerously empower our terrorist enemies by allowing them to choose agents of an "innocent" background that will guarantee them only a casual investigation. It may cause enough anger among those of similar backgrounds to those selected to increase the support by nations or individuals for our enemies abroad or reduce the support for government efforts to obtain critical intelligence at home or abroad. E-mail lists of many thousands are provided very current notice of any such activity.

How such selection could help is also clear. Take the problem of suicide bombers. As I have noted, we know that close to 100 percent of that category come from one of a handful of groups—most of which have never used terrorism against the United States. The only groups using suicide bombers against the United States are Arabs acting on behalf of Palestinian causes and radical fundamentalist Muslim terrorists.[31] Combined, these groups constitute a very small percentage of foreign nationals residing in or seeking to visit the United States. Denying these groups access to targets or particular resources until we have developed increased information about the applicant will therefore impose a small fraction of the costs and inconvenience that would be generated if such measures were applied to the entire population.

By concentrating on these groups the government can carry out a better-focused and more intensive investigation as a precondition of access. The lower costs and greater potential efficacy are true even if the odds are extremely high that any particular visiting Arab, Muslim fundamentalist, or recent visitor to Pakistan is 100 percent opposed to the terrorism. Even if it is unfair to suspect any randomly chosen member of the group, it might be effective to concentrate the attention we give to the problem of suicide bombers on all members of the group. That depends on the balance of benefits to our security from the measures against the costs.

For these reasons efficiency, at least in the short term, may dictate concentrating on limited sub-categories of the populations, even with the knowledge that the number of false positives (innocent members subjected to investigation or denial of access) will vastly exceed the number of legitimate suspects. We have done that by insisting on more elaborate investigations of young males applying to visit the United States from any of a number of Arab countries.

But against what may be the net gains in security we have to balance heretofore unconsidered costs in freedom and unity. Every member of the class denied access or subjected to special investigation before being granted access to a place or resources will be made to feel less than an equal in the United States. So will the other nationals of his home country. If that message about some individuals is conveyed to all our citizens, it will also encourage private forms of discrimination. Such costs have been experienced by Catholics in Northern Ireland and Arabs in Israel.[32] The measures have reduced the level of local support in pursuing terrorists in both places.

The issue of profiling is also complicated by the variety of categories that might be used to allocate special investigative attention or greater care in granting access to likely targets or resources. At one extreme, applying selective measures to Arab-American or Muslim American citizens would impose wholly unwarranted costs on them and on the unity of our country. At the other extreme, it is too late, and the practice too common, to complain effectively about aliens being treated differently in these regards as they enter the United States. Within the United States, either all non-citizens or only those who are temporarily visiting and are not residents could be subject to special attention. We could give special attention to those who were from, or have passports showing recent visits to, particular countries. For citizens as well as visitors, we might pay special attention to members of, or those attending, more radical mosques. We could, of course, focus on any combination of these categories.

Each of these choices has its own particular dangers. Whatever category defines our special attention also conveys suspicion of disloyalty, as well as the risks of special investigation and the costs of at least temporary denial of access to places or resources that others can access freely. Those belonging to whatever category is chosen are likely to avoid any situation where the category is likely to be applied or, in the case of categorization by voluntarily chosen political or religious groups, forego the choice that leads to the investigation. If government officials choose a broader category, they reduce the burdens and embarrassment to each member of the group but increase the number of members burdened at all. If a category is too broad—for example, doing a careful airport frisk of people randomly chosen from among air travelers, including 80-year-old grandmothers with their grandchildren— the effort brings ridicule along with its wasted effort.

2. SPYING ON CERTAIN RELIGIOUS AND POLITICAL GROUPS

The use of informants, which the law does not limit, is always likely to create a substantial inhibition of democratic political activity. When the Justice Department mistakenly suspected the Committee in Solidarity with the People of El Salvador (CISPES) of supporting Salvadorian terrorists, the U.S. Senate described the resulting danger to democratic values in this way:

> The American people have the right to disagree with the policies of their government, to support unpopular political causes, and to associate with others in the peaceful expression of those views, without fear of investigation by the FBI or any other government agency. As Justice Lewis Powell wrote in the *Keith* case, "The price of lawful public dissent must not be a dread of subjection to an unchecked surveillance power."
>
> . . .Unjustified investigations of political expression and dissent can have a debilitating effect upon our political system. When people see that this can happen, they become wary of associating with groups that disagree with the government and more wary of what they say and write. The impact is to undermine the effectiveness of popular self-government. If the people are inhibited in expressing their views, a nation's government becomes increasingly divorced from the will of its citizens.[33]

To avoid that inhibition of speech, recent attorneys general have required a reasonable suspicion that violence is being planned before authorizing any domestic intelligence-gathering to prevent terrorism without a foreign connection.[34] The classified standards for opening an investigation of international terrorism are said also to require a factual basis.[35] These standards are believed to follow closely the definition of a foreign party or agent in the Foreign Intelligence Surveillance Act: someone acting on behalf of a foreign power or group to further international terrorism. True, in both cases the required predicate is somewhat elastic. In times of great danger, it will be stretched in the direction of monitoring whatever groups vocally support a state or group engaged in terrorism. Such speech, even though it is a weak sign, is often the only open indication that someone is more likely than others to engage in terrorist activities.

Attorney General Ashcroft has modified the guidelines for investigating domestic terrorism in two quite defensible ways. FBI agents are now permitted to attend *public* meetings and to surf the Internet without needing to have any prior basis of suspicion. This conforms to the more general rule that law enforcement officers are allowed to go wherever private individuals can go without trespassing. The Attorney General is also reducing any special protection of religious or political meetings.

The case for these changes is strong but it deserves discussion. In making these decisions, the Justice Department showed no recognition of the real costs they involve. People leading or attending one of the 1,200 or so mosques in the United States will be deeply concerned about what they say if they believe that an FBI agent may be present. The same is true of people attending pro-Palestinian meetings. The attorney general's change in quarter-century-old arrangements may be right, but it is not so straightforward as not to require discussion. The right to attend open meetings also carries with it the right to create files. In 1975, FBI headquarters held more than a half a million such files, many on organizations we now recognize to be entirely legitimate. The order that Attorney General Ashcroft modified was intended by Attorney General Edward Levi in the Ford administration to correct that situation. We are now undoing it.

3. DIMINISHING PRIVACY AND ANONYMITY OF EVERYONE

The third alternative (to profiling and to spying on groups) is to use the capacity of high-powered computers to combine readily available pieces of information that are not based on ethnicity and thereby select the subgroup on whom investigations will focus. Germany has adopted this method. The object—to produce a large number of investigative files that can be used to deny access or to incapacitate—has its own serious costs.

For restriction of access to targets or resources and for monitoring the activities of suspects, this option would eliminate the costs of apparent discrimination, but the costs to civil liberties still would be great. Unless protections of privacy were carefully built into the system—and perhaps even then—every individual in America would have to anticipate: (1) a larger file of personal information kept by the government combining information from a number of public and private agencies; (2) more frequent government checks of this file; (3) a reduced ability to separate oneself from one's own recorded personal history; and (4) a system of checking an individual's identity against recorded files that is designed to make records of the individual's new activities whenever old records are checked.

In creating new files for preventive purposes, we will be changing the traditional balance between law enforcement and internal security and the cultures associated with each. Almost every other nation in the world has an internal security agency that is separate from its law enforcement agency, freed from many civil liberties constraints, and charged with providing the information the government needs (or the chief executive wants) for policy and political decisions, as well as for prevention of dangerous situations. The United States has not created an agency with such broad discretion, instead giving only the Federal Bureau of Investigation an internal intelligence function and, even then, narrowing that responsibility to merely counter-terrorism and counter-espionage activities. But, as Chapter 7 explores, our level of acceptance of domestic intelligence activities has changed and will continue to change.

Three Specific Proposals So Far Unconsidered Because of Constitutional Concerns

1. SURVEILLANCE POWERS REGARDING VISITING ALIENS

The proper level of protection of foreign visitors from intrusive surveillance is far from clear. There is much to be said for an amendment to the Foreign Intelligence Surveillance Act (FISA) to permit intelligence surveillance of non-U.S. persons (i.e., temporary visitors to the United States) on reasonable suspicion that they fall into those categories in the act that describe international terrorists. "Reasonable suspicion" requires less than the present standard of "probable cause," and thus would allow additional protection against terrorist activity by visitors from abroad without interfering with the rights of people permanently living in the United States. It is stricter than the standard we are applying in denying admission to the United States.

When we have reasonable suspicion that someone is "visiting" the United States to engage in terrorism against us, we need to gather information about his or her plans and associates. There are three options. (1) The FBI can use visual observation of activities or other forms of less intrusive surveillance for some sustained period in the hope of building enough "probable cause" for a far more promising use of electronic surveillance or physical search under FISA. (2) We can often arrest the visitor for a violation of the immigration laws and question him while in detention. (3) Finally, with the proposed amendment, we could use the FISA statute to discover the plans and associates of any visitor we had good reason to suspect was involved in international terrorism. The first is slow and ineffective, especially if the visitor is careful not to provide additional evidence by hiding his activities while in the United States. The second assumes implausibly that non-coercive interrogation will prove fruitful in most cases and will not dangerously alert colleagues. The third is by far the most promising.

Electronic surveillance is also likely to be far less disruptive of the individual's life than is our recent detention of hundreds of suspects on immigration charges. Indeed, the total interference with the visitor's civil liberties is limited. There is very little of the most serious risk: government spying on those seeking to exercise democratic political liberties. The visitor will rarely be playing any role in our democratic process. While he is visiting within the United States, there will be a very real impact on the visitor's privacy rights, but the loss of privacy is temporary and the situation—visiting a foreign country—is one where expectations of privacy are low.

While the matter of constitutionality is far from certain, there is a very good chance that the Supreme Court would sustain the change under the reasoning of its decision in *United States vs. Verdugo-Urquidez*.[36] The standard that was applied in that case, to allow the search abroad of the home of an alien in U.S. prison, was whether the alien has "come within the territory of the United States and developed substantial connections with the country." The Supreme Court would be likely to conclude that an investigation focused on a visitor reasonably believed to be coming to the United States to attack it would not be an investigation of someone with the "substantial connections with the country" that are required for full Fourth Amendment protection. Chief Justice William Rehnquist wrote for the Court that full protection is available only to "the people"—"a class of persons who are part of a national community." Any challenge to the amendments would be particularly unlikely to succeed in the case of anyone who entered the country without permission.

2. AN "INCITEMENT" OFFENSE

Section 12 of the United Kingdom's Terrorism Act makes it a criminal offense for a person to incite another person to commit an act of terrorism, even outside the United Kingdom, and to invite support for a proscribed organization. Other, older legislation makes incitement an offense if intended or likely to stir up racial hatred. Israel, like France, has even broader prohibitions, defined in the Prevention of Terrorism Ordinance No. 33 of 5708-1948. Under the ordinance, a person who "publishes, in writing or orally, words of praise, sympathy or encouragement for acts of violence...or [who] publishes, in writing or orally, words of praise or sympathy or an appeal for aid or support of a terrorist organization" is guilty of a criminal offense.[37] Israel has in fact outlawed incitements to racism, but under a different law (Sec. 144B(A) of the Penal Law (Penal Law, 1986, 38 L.S.I. 230, (1986))): "Any person who publishes anything for the purposes of racist incitement shall be liable to five years imprisonment." In Section 144A, racism is defined as "persecution, humiliation, denigration, expression of hatred, threats or violence, or promoting feelings of ill will and resentment toward a community or sections of the population, solely due to color or belonging to a particular race or national-ethnic origin."[38] Israel's laws apply even when the speech does not explicitly incite violence, but merely praises past acts of violence. There is no need to prove that the incitement would lead to violence or racism, only that it was intended to.

For many months, the British felt unable to use their incitement law effectively against even such advocates of mass violence as the leader of the Finsbury Park Mosque, Abu-Hamzi al Masri, who had argued that it is acceptable to kill Westerners in Muslim countries, praised the attacks on the World Trade Center, and called for a much broader "holy war." The much broader Israeli statutes easily forbid this activity.

Some of our nation's founders, in particular President John Adams, experimented, soon after the First Amendment was ratified, with a statute that made it a crime to "conspire to oppose any measure of the government" or defame the president. The United States has taken from this unhappy experiment and later wartime experiences the lesson that speech should be left far more uninhibited. In the controlling precedent of *Brandenburg vs. Ohio*, 395 US 444 (1969), Ohio applied a statute criminalizing advocacy of "unlawful methods of terrorism as a means of . . . political reform," to members of the Ku Klux Klan who engaged in defamatory speech against, and urged "getting," blacks and Jews. The court held Ohio's law unconstitutional, stating that speech can be forbidden only if it incites imminent lawless action and is also likely to produce that action. Mere advocacy cannot be punished. The Second Circuit Court of Appeals applied that ruling but was still able to affirm the conviction of Sheik Omar Abdel Rahman for seditious conspiracy, making no exception for religious speech.[39]

The Bush administration has not sought to press these lines. Indeed, it is unlikely that speech satisfying British standards is in fact occurring publicly and with frequency. Even sermons intended to inspire action, perhaps in support of the Palestinian cause, are likely to be carefully expressed. But the constitutional protections do not prevent our making it a crime, as we have, to knowingly give material support to an organization that is promoting terrorist causes. And they may not prevent criminalizing the dissemination of information intended to help others in committing a crime by, for example, publishing instructions on how to commit a terrorist attack.[40] Nor does the *Brandenburg* holding prevent punishment of speech that threatens violence.[41]

The most useful function of any such law might be its extraterritorial reach to those abroad inciting violence against the United States or its citizens. The "protective principle" of international law may well authorize such a statute. With that reach, and with the consent of the state where the speaker resides, the U.S. could itself act against those urging violence in or against the United States. Without such consent, however, many states would doubtless refuse to extradite offenders, relying on the "political offense" exception found in extradition treaties.

3. Membership Crimes

Finally, an alternative to preventive detention even where criminal activity cannot be proved, and to detention after arrest for some frequently committed crime which is rarely prosecuted, would be to continue the requirement of proof beyond a reasonable doubt, but to make the crime one that is far easier to prove. The "membership" crimes take this approach. Unfortunately, making a crime far easier to prove generally means making it, at the same time, far easier to commit without actions manifesting serious, harmful intentions.

The United Kingdom forbids membership in proscribed organizations so long as the organization was proscribed when the individual joined and the individual has "taken part in the activities of the organization at any time [since] it was proscribed."[42] Israel's Prevention of Terrorism Ordinance No. 33 (PTN) broadly states that "a person who is a member of a terrorist organization shall be guilty of an offense."

Both of these standards are broader than present U.S. law, which requires almost all the elements of a traditional conspiracy. For this reason, crimes of membership in the Communist Party were sharply restricted in 1961 by the Supreme Court's decision in *Scales vs. United States* 367 U.S. 203 (1961). The court permitted prosecution for membership in illegal groups only if the member is "active, has guilty knowledge, and intends to further the illegal purposes of the group." It did not permit prosecution of "the mere voluntary listing of names on [a group's] rolls."

Coercive Interrogation

The administration has shown unexplained and untraditional preferences for coercive interrogation over electronic and other surveillance as a way of learning about the plans and associates of someone suspected of terrorism. It has authorized coercion short of torture for non-citizens outside the United States in forms Israel has found illegal. It has sent foreign suspects to states that freely torture. What about authorizing torture within the United States of citizens as well as non-citizens? The answer is to go the other way and abandon a new bad practice.

Authorizing torture even to obtain information that can save lives is a very bad and dangerous idea that can easily be made to sound plausible. There is a subtle fallacy embedded in the traditional "ticking bomb" argument for the use of torture to save lives. That argument goes like this. First, many of us can imagine dangers so dire that we might torture or kill guilty or innocent persons if we were quite sure that was necessary and sufficient to prevent those dangers. Indeed, most citizens feel this way, although differing in the circumstances and the certainty level they would want. Therefore, the "ticking bomb" argument concludes, most of us want a "system" for authorizing torture or murder; we need only debate the circumstances and the level of certainty. What isn't acceptable, the argument goes, is to make torture illegal and yet expect our intelligence agencies to use it in dire circumstances or to hide it abroad.

This conclusion, leading to abandonment of one of the few worldwide legal prohibitions, leaves out the fact that there is far too little reason to have faith in an intelligence-based authorizing system for reliably finding the circumstances required for torture. The primary reason is simple: the costs of torture are borne by the suspect tortured, not by those who decide to torture him; the costs of a bomb going off are borne by those whose careers depend on not overlooking any grave danger. The conclusion also ignores the very high probability that the practice of torture will spread unwisely if acceptance of torture, even if only with the approval of judges, is substituted for a flat, worldwide prohibition.

Take the recommendation of my colleague Alan Dershowitz for judicially issued "torture warrants" to substitute for torture at the discretion of intelligence agents pursuing a "ticking bomb."[43] It will increase the use of torture. Any law enforcement or intelligence official who tortures a prisoner in the United States now is very likely to be prosecuted and imprisoned. Punches may be thrown, but anything we think of as "torture" is considered an inexcusable practice. Now, highly coercive interrogation with physical violence is a crime, at least unless after the fact the interrogator can demonstrate that he reasonably believed torture was the only way to avoid even worse consequences in a situation where the legislature would have wanted an exception to its prohibition of torture. This is also the rule in Israel.

Professor Dershowitz proposes to instead make torture acceptable and legal whenever a judge accepts the judgment of intelligence officials, before the torture, that: (1) there is a bomb in a public place; (2) the suspect knows where it is; (3) torture will get the truth, not a false story, out of him before the bomb explodes; *and* (4) the bomb won't be moved in the meantime. Professor Dershowitz wants to bet that judges will say "no" in a high enough percentage of cases of "ticking bombs" that whatever moral force their refusal has will offset the legitimating and demoralizing effects of authorizing occasional torture. It is a bad bet. Judges have deferred to the last fourteen thousand requests for national security wiretaps and they would defer here.[44] The basis of their decisions, information revealing secret "sources and methods" of intelligence-gathering, would not be public. And if the judge refused, overrode the judgment of agents who thought lives would be lost without torture, and denied a warrant, why would that decision be more likely to be accepted and followed by agents desperate to save lives than the flat ban on torture we now have?

Some officials in the CIA have expressed interest in the proposal. They haven't asked how many false positives we would be prepared to accept. Simple probability theory shows that we would get 6 false positives (failure to save lives) out of 10 occasions of torture even in the extraordinarily unlikely event that the intelligence officers convince the judge that they were really 80 percent sure of each of the above four predictions.[45] And even if we would tolerate this number of false positives if torture were in fact the only way to get the needed information to defuse the bomb, there are frequently other promising ways (such as emergency searches or stimulating conversations over tapped phones) that will be abandoned or discounted if torture is available (and, to some torturers, satisfying). Finally, if we approve torture in one set of circumstances, isn't every country then free to define its own exceptions, applicable to Americans as well as its own citizens? Fear of that led us to accept the Geneva Convention prohibiting torture of a prisoner of war although obtaining his information might save dozens of American lives.

As to a long-term strategy for dealing with terrorists, torture is an even worse idea. Many believe that public revulsion at the government's use of torture was responsible for the French loss of Algeria.[46] Coercive questioning may well have increased commitment to a terror campaign in Northern Ireland. And how would the U.S. public react to viewing or hearing about the treatment of the first three innocent Americans tortured by our government? How supportive of the FBI would they be after reading this? We might, to avoid these consequences, find informal ways to concentrate torture among those somehow "different" from most of us. But that is worse still. Torture is a prescription for losing a war for support of our beliefs in the hope of reducing the casualties from relatively small battles.

Conclusion

No one can persuasively decide how much fear and anger is sensible for a proud people to feel in the aftermath of September 11. What we can say is that steps taken in response to fear should be well calculated to actually reduce the danger; that the steps taken in response to anger should be directed at the right people; and that the value Americans place on individual rights, decency, and liberty should be considered alongside our fear and anger.

No one can speak for all of us in deciding the trade-offs, when some departure from tradition is justified, among equal protection of the laws, privacy and the fearless exercise of democratic freedoms. We can, however, demand careful, frank and considered calculation in balancing the trade-offs regarding ethnic profiling, use of informants in religious and political groups, and keeping more files and more easily accessible file retrieval systems. In making these decisions, we must recognize that powerful and legitimate concerns will be at risk whichever way we go.

Similarly, there is something imponderable about comparing the dangers of a presidential assertion of power to bypass the courts and use the military to detain, sentence, and execute non-citizens with the risks that very dangerous individuals will be left among us or that our treasured secrets will be revealed at trial. However, we can make sure that we assess accurately the capacity of our courts to deal with these risks and not take the easy road, surrendering some of our most basic liberties unnecessarily to any president's unshared power.

To all these immeasurables, we should also add the trade-off, discussed in Chapter 4, between the safety of Americans and the liberty of those abroad facing despotic regimes doing, or pretending to do, our bidding. What we must do is assure that no one assumes the American people would willingly buy a small amount of increased safety in exchange for the torture, detention, or imprisonment of innocents abroad.

In sum, the gravest danger to civil liberties and human rights emerging in the aftermath of September 11 is that leaders will think we are without concern for non-citizens within the United States, indifferent to the welfare of people repressed by despotic governments, prepared to accept without question unequal treatment based on ethnicity, and unable or unwilling to see that there must be trade-offs even among our own freedoms. An American people encouraged to earn the respect for our traditions and values will be left with very hard choices. That is inevitable. But we should seek to make these choices proudly and intelligently, and not out of fear and anger alone.

Chapter 6

Building the Future Internationally

The very notion of "war" is intended to suggest urgency and a priority that supervenes most other claimants for attention in our domestic and foreign policy, and that leads us to belittle even the arrangements thought necessary for democracy in more ordinary times. But this single-mindedness inevitably threatens the future both with the effects of changes made in the name of the "war" and with the effects of disregard for other concerns because of preoccupation with that "war." I have argued in the preceding chapter that an intelligent policy to deal with the threat of terrorism requires consideration not only of the dollar cost of proposed policies but also of their cost in terms of democratic values. An important and closely related point requires considering the future as we deal with the present and, in particular, our future place in the world.

Fifteen months after September 11, a poll by the Pew Global Attitudes Project showed that regard for the United States had dropped, since the year 2000, 17 percentage points in Germany, 8 in Britain, 6 in Italy. By June 2003, Pew polls showed favorable opinions of the United States had slipped over the past year "in nearly every country for which trend measures are available" and "majorities in five of seven NATO countries surveyed support a more independent relationship with the United States on diplomatic and security affairs." But should we care?

That we need the continuing ability to address other policies at home and abroad without being blinded by our concerns about terrorism can be demonstrated by a mental experiment. Imagine what we would want for the United States in the year 2015 and maybe long before that. We would want our democratic politics and our notions of civil liberties and civil rights to be much like what we have enjoyed for many decades. That means, for one thing, that we would hope all significant executive policies, including policies with regard to terrorism, were subject to vigorous oversight by congressional committees and that the most important enjoyed debate on the floor of Congress and in the public. We would want both citizens and others who live in the United States (resident aliens) to feel free to engage in public debate—short of urging violence—without fear of detention, intensive monitoring, or denial of access to places and facilities available to other citizens. We would want the United States to continue our policies of freedom of religion and equal protection, finding some way to be both secure and welcoming of Muslims and Arabs (and any other identifiable religious or ethnic group with which the then-current terrorists were associated).

These understandings about what it is to live in America may or may not be as important as having, by that future date, adequate security against devastating attacks. Reconciling these demands means we would need, by that future date, an ability to distinguish sharply in the cost we were prepared to bear between massive attacks and more easily mounted small-scale attacks of the sort we saw in the 1980s; and we would need to be able to distinguish between irregular, sporadic attacks and painfully enduring campaigns. Many of the steps necessary to stop completely even a relatively low level of sporadic attacks on Americans around the world are too costly, and too unlikely to succeed, to justify abandoning fundamental democratic liberties.

Outside our borders we would want a friendlier world with which to deal. We would also want a world economy safe for investment—growing, and fair to all its participants. We would want to have a position of leadership with allies who are willing to cooperate freely as well as when put under intense pressure. And we would want many dangerous activities to be restrained by an effective form of international law.

Among parts of the Muslim population and other opponents of modernization and globalization we would want a greatly diminished level of hatred of the United States. In that world made up of those who feel left behind by Western technology, prosperity, and power we would want more democratic, economically healthy societies. We believe such societies to be safer for us as well as better for their citizens.

I may have left out important characteristics of the world we would like to see in 10 or 15 years. But my point does not depend upon the completeness of my list. It is that we have to consider the effects of our decisions and actions in the present on the future, not only because they will affect our likely capacity to deal with terrorism in the future but, even more important, because they help to determine the desirability of the society we will enjoy in a very few years.

How do present activities affect that future? They create precedents at home. President Roosevelt's use of military tribunals against German saboteurs formed the basis for President Bush's claim of the same authority 60 years later. Accepting President Bush's claim of a presidential right to detain indefinitely, without access to courts, American citizens arrested for supporting terrorism in the United States,[1] on the ground that they are associated with foreign terrorists, relies in part on the precedent of his own, barely contested, prior claim of the right to detain resident aliens.

Our decisions with respect to international law and permissible practice legitimize certain activities at least to the extent of effectively preventing our complaining in the future about actions by others. Secretly paying Iran for the return of hostages held by the Hezbollah[2] prevented us from effectively criticizing similar concessions by allies. If we justify our attack on Iraq by claiming there is a severe risk that it is building weapons of mass destruction, so may any of the five nations with veto power on the Security Council use preemptive attacks and, until the Security Council acts, so may Israel or Syria, India or Pakistan. After we claim, as Defense Secretary Rumsfeld has, the power to send assassination teams into other countries to deal with those we have concluded threaten our security,[3] so can other nations. These judgments will become legitimate in the sense of being free from the condemnation of the world's only superpower. Our power of effective condemnation is not trivial; it is well worth preserving.

Our influence in the future is also shaped by our reputation among our allies. That, in turn, is determined in part by a very long history but in part by the more salient activities we engage in currently. For leadership, reputation is critical: reputation for wisdom, for steadfastness, for boldness in using economic and political powers, for willingness to share decision-making in the world, and for caring for those who feel left behind. The rapid U.S. flight from Lebanon and Somalia after loss of American lives showed a lack of steadfastness, and offered our enemies hope as a recruiting issue.

One crucial part of national reputation is bilateral. Trust in keeping commitments can be created or dissipated over time. North Korea hemorrhaged trust in October 2002 when it admitted breaking its commitment not to seek nuclear weapons. A major barrier to some form of peaceful resolution of the struggle between Israelis and Palestinians is that both sides have squandered whatever trust there was in the willingness of the other to comply with the terms necessary for agreement, such as an end to terrorism or an end to the settlement policy.[4]

These are only some of the ways that our actions now bear on both our capacities in the future and the very nature of the society and world in which we will live. The simple point is that the future has to be considered as we deal with terrorism now. Of course what we do now will facilitate or harm our ability to deal with terrorism in the future. But even more important, what we do now about terrorism will affect American society in the future as well as the nature of the society of nations and peoples with which the United States will share a shrinking planet.

The Conditions for Continuing World Leadership

Look in more detail at the impact of our leadership actions today on the place of the United States in the world in the years ahead. The United States is not running for "most popular nation." Five factors other than popularity cause us to be concerned about what Jefferson called, in the first sentence of our Declaration of Independence, "a decent respect to the opinions of mankind." (1) We need international cooperation to accomplish many of our most important purposes in the world. In particular, we need a variety of forms of cooperation with a number of nations to increase our safety against the type of attacks to which we are now most vulnerable: terrorist attacks. (2) To avoid needless and dangerous national conflicts, to manage a global economy, and to protect our citizens, we need widespread respect for international law. (3) If we are to lead the set of friendly nations committed to democracy and free economies, our strategic judgments must be respected. (4) As a condition of our own power at home and as a highly important form of influence we have on populations abroad, we need a capacity to lead that goes beyond calculations and claims commitment to an ideology or morality (such as democracy, law, and free private economies) to which others will be drawn. (5) Whether or not it is useful to us—and it probably is—we do and should care about democracy, human rights, and a decent standard of living in other countries of the world whose people are no less "endowed by their creator with certain unalienable rights" among which are "life, liberty, and the pursuit of happiness."

The lack of support—the occasionally open hostility—among allies and Arab states for our invasion of Iraq in 2003 raises the question: should these relations to and with other nations and peoples really concern us, the world's only superpower? Consider what these relationships mean in just one policy area: terrorism.

We will not be able to discover who is plotting against us without the cooperation of foreign governments. A well-documented example of this was our effort to investigate who was responsible for a truck bomb explosion at the Khobar Towers military base in Saudi Arabia.[5] There, the FBI struggled in a complicated world of Middle East politics where evidence available to Saudi Arabia pointed to the responsibility of Iran. Fearing that our response to obtaining that evidence would be an attack on Iran, the Saudis tried to avoid what they anticipated would then be retaliation by Iran against Saudi Arabia. What evidence we could obtain necessarily depended on permission to investigate within Saudi Arabia—an activity that is forbidden by international and national laws unless consent is first obtained. Obtaining that consent—something never fully accomplished—depended upon a network of cooperative relations between the Saudis and us.

It is true that a superpower can often obtain cooperation from other nations by paying for it, or threatening harm if it is not furnished. Why then should it worry about proposing plans which are of mutual benefit, or entering into a regime of formal or informal partnership under which one state foregoes advantages now in the expectation that the other will reciprocate over time? The United States has immense capacity to use the first two forms of influence, but having only these arrows in our quiver has some major disadvantages. Neither what we offer to Egypt or Saudi Arabia or Turkey nor the force of our threats against Libya or Iraq can generate enthusiastic commitment. In these ways we can at best get what we bargain for and not what we later find that we need. Leadership in a common cause or a partnership promises the richer benefits that come with the other state actually wanting our plans to succeed or the United States as a nation to prosper.

By bargaining and threatening we also only get what we can observe; we are not protected against defaults we cannot detect. Professor Mark Kleiman of UCLA names this phenomenon after W. C. Fields. Fields's Law is, Kleiman says, "any incentive to create a result also creates an incentive to simulate the same result." A corollary is that "to maintain a given level of reliability, the resources invested in verifying any performance measure need to rise roughly in proportion to the stakes involved." The stakes are extraordinarily high for the nations we hope to induce to act against popular and dangerous terrorist groups within their midst. "To manage," Kleiman continues, one must be able, "not only to measure, but to measure in the face of active impression management among those measured." There is an alternative: cooperation through creating a real belief in shared goals.

Although we are a superpower, we also need respect for international law if we are going to obtain the cooperation of even our closest friends in prosecuting terrorists who operate against the United States from abroad or who flee abroad after an operation. A state that is not already threatened by a terrorist group takes unwanted risks of becoming a victim itself when it helps us punish our attackers. Reciprocally binding treaties help overcome this hurdle. Bilateral cooperation through treaties is just part of the story. We benefit from close to a dozen multilateral agreements prohibiting everything from biological warfare to attacks on diplomats, or the use of explosives in terrorist attacks.[6] Openly disregarding such treaties turns even an unfriendly state into a pariah; and so even such states have reason to comply.

To the extent to which we can bring together the major democracies and the major economies of the world behind a common effort to deal with dangers from terrorism, to defuse a potential conflict between India and Pakistan, or to battle organized crime and corruption, we can enjoy the benefits of concerted activity rather than the inefficiency and inconveniences of every major nation going its own way. But for that we need to enjoy the confidence of others in both the fairness of the processes with which joint decisions are made and the wisdom of what we urge.[7] If we lose the confidence of others, we will lose much of our capacity to lead.

Great power can lead to great resentment as readily as to admiration. The anger at our invasion of Iraq demonstrates that. We have to compete for public support around the world in terms of our vision and our example, as well as in terms of our wealth, technology, and military power. Ideology is the area in which radical fundamentalist Islamists are openly challenging us. Over time, it matters greatly whether American society is regarded as a role model of multi-ethnic tolerance, lawfulness, democracy, and technological initiative, or whether it is thought of as simply a powerful, wealthy, self-interested empire. If we are a role model, political forces throughout the world will identify with us and will support our initiatives. If our strength is thought to be solely in wealth and armaments, we will inspire secret opposition and even terrorism.

The final reason we care about the opinions of mankind is the simplest: American citizens do and, because of our advantages, should care about the well-being of others outside our nation's boundaries. Human rights and economic development are the primary areas of concern. Giving force to our concerns through treaties and discretionary decisions contributes to moral leadership but it also expresses a legitimate—and admirable—generosity.

The Effects of Today's Counterterrorism Policy on These Relationships and on Our Future Leadership

Many of the benefits of international leadership, cooperation, and law depend upon relationships and impressions that endure for some period of time. Thus, like other matters of reputation, they do not change rapidly and, also like other matters of reputation, they have immense practical importance. The way we choose to handle terrorism at home and abroad will bear importantly on our place in the world in the years ahead, although our power and wealth and the interdependence they create protect us for now against any abrupt changes in our capacity to influence other nations.

Our counterterrorism programs either consume or build capital in the foreign policy area; and that area is, in the long run, extremely important to our well-being. There are innumerable ways in which we can build or undermine the cooperation and the trust we will need in the long run to deal with terrorism. Some we have tried; others have merely been considered. Some are addressed to our close allies; others, to our opponents. The Bush administration has, on the whole, been consuming—not building—that intangible capital.

THE IMPORTANCE OF UNDERSTANDING AND SUPPORTING EACH OTHER'S GOALS REGARDING TERRORISM

If we do not make a good-faith effort to arrive at collective positions with our closest allies, we will lose their cooperation over time. The issue may be a discrete one such as the invasion of Iraq or blocking the International Criminal Court. It may be as broad as an overall conception of the threat and the best approaches to dealing with it.

In a militarily brilliant but diplomatically inane response to the seizure of the *Achille Lauro* in 1985, the United States safely forced down an Egyptian airliner carrying the terrorists on Italian territory where we tried to seize the terrorists by military action without the consent of the Italians. By the time we were through, the Italian government had fallen (not an unusual event in those days) amid denunciations of our unilateral disregard of both duties to allies and international law.

The simple fact, undetected by our highest counter-terrorism officials, was that Italy's belief about how to deal with hostage taking (build widespread international criticism that isolates the terrorist politically and negotiate to save lives) was very different from ours (use armed rescue operations and never negotiate). Broader questions about what terrorism was all about were some of the factors behind the disagreement. For the United States, it was a moral challenge and a chance to show that our military capacities and strategies were not helpless when faced with terrorist tactics. For the Italians it was a small part of a political/military struggle for a Palestinian cause in which many of their loyalties were on the side of the Palestinians.

The same sort of difference over the threat of terrorism exists today with regard to our allies. It is rooted in differences in location, likelihood of being an international target, history with terrorism, history with internal security measures, political pressures, and more. Not just Italy but even such close allies as Germany and Japan have a view of September 11 which is very different from ours.[8]

For Germany, counterterrorism policy requires a balance between never permitting again the weakness that undermined the Weimar Republic and never permitting again the excesses of the Gestapo. The Germans see the danger of terrorism largely in terms of internal threats but value external cooperation as a less threatening form of governmental response. Germany limits sharply its ways of gathering private information but compensates with highly sophisticated ways of combining bits of quasi-public information. In light of its history, Germany is unenthusiastic about participation in military operations such as the second war with Iraq, although it has participated actively in the investigative aftermath of September 11.

Since September 11, Germany has substantially increased the powers of its domestic intelligence agency and its police to investigate groups using Germany as a base for attacking other countries, but this has not been uncontested.[9] There has not been a Muslim terrorist attack in Germany in more than 15 years. We have to recognize these differences, for they bear importantly on attitudes toward "a war on terrorism," although so do long and powerful economic and political alliances with the United States.

For Japan, September 11 was a very remote threat, an occasion for showing a greater willingness to bear a greater part of the burden after it was criticized for its limited involvement in the 1991 Persian Gulf War. As in Germany, our "war" creates a challenge to long-hallowed policies, powerfully supported domestically, limiting the military involvement of Japan since World War II. Japan had successfully forced its Red Army terrorists outside of Japan. It reacted with remarkable calm both to the seizure of the Japanese Embassy in Lima, Peru, and to the chemical attacks by the Aum Shinrikyo group.

For Japan, terrorism belongs with drugs, refugees, and natural disasters as something to be dealt with when it occurs, an approach that assures that there will be no return to the dangerous powers of the police and the military before 1945. The heart of the Japanese way of dealing with terrorism is maintaining a very close police contact with the population. Traditionally it has been willing to pay ransoms, understanding of the causes of terrorism, and disinclined to think of terrorism as a global problem.

Cooperation with even such close allies as Germany and Japan will depend upon a major effort to reconcile different definitions of the threat, ideas about how to deal with it, and concerns about risks to democratic values.

THE ADVANTAGES OF DISPLAYING RESPECT FOR INTERNATIONAL LAW, STEADFASTNESS AND WISDOM IN FIGHTING TERRORISM

If we adopt a policy of sending American Special Operations Forces abroad to assassinate those who appear to be leaders of terrorist groups, as Defense Secretary Rumsfeld suggested,[10] we will sacrifice a great power—the effect of stern U.S. condemnation of similar practices by, for example, Iran. The same is true when we define for ourselves too generously our rights to make war under the UN charter (for example, in Iraq); or assess too carelessly who is threatening us (as we did in bombing Sudan after the attacks on our East African embassies).

We have some admirable history in this area. President Reagan courageously released highly classified intelligence information to explain the bombing of Libya in 1985. In 1993, President Clinton delayed for weeks a response against Iraq for an assassination attempt against past President George H. W. Bush while the facts as to responsibility were double-checked by the FBI and the Justice Department.

If our strategic judgments about handling an Islamist challenge are to be respected by our allies, we need far more consistent and broader strategies in the area. We encouraged Hezbollah by responding to its attacks on our soldiers and embassy in Lebanon by abandoning Lebanon; and later we further encouraged terrorists by pulling out of Somalia under small-scale attack. At both times our declared policies forbade any compromise with terrorism. We have failed to show the steadfastness and the wisdom that would cause others to follow us not only in individual cases but, more broadly, in our overall strategy toward terrorism. We showed foolish optimism and reckless inconsistency in trading missiles for hostages Iran controlled after promising never to make concessions for hostages. We have recklessly allowed Saudi Arabia freedom to support members of an Islamist Jihad against us.[11] On a wider field, we have seemed willing to tie our entire foreign policy to a single issue, terrorism. Leadership among our allies requires a broader base. And it requires listening to them and sharing responsibility for decisions and actions.

MORAL LEADERSHIP AS A CONDITION OF POLITICAL LEADERSHIP

Our moral and ideological leadership requires us to be a model of democracy at home, even under threat. Creating military tribunals, limiting access to attorneys, allowing detention without trial—all have been tried and rejected by our allies. For moral leadership we have to try to export an ideology of democracy and rule of law. Supporting undemocratic regimes that use powerful internal security agencies to control their peoples undermines our ability to reach populations that might otherwise want to imitate our ways of governing—democratic and lawful ways that have been so successful. Our ability to encourage foreign trade depends upon being sure it is of advantage to populations whose governments may be corrupt and whose businesses may think competition at home is not at all what they need.

The morality of our actions abroad, no less than those at home, is a condition of political leadership. This, as well as the concerns of our own citizens for human rights, means that we cannot solve the problem of terrorism by exporting violations of human rights that we would not tolerate at home. As we have seen in Chapter 4, we could in fact reduce the immediate danger to Americans at the cost of ignoring the liberties and rights of others promised by the United Nations' Universal Declaration of Human Rights and the International Covenant on Civil and Political Rights. But the long-term cost of this is to cease to be a model admired, and thus followed, among the populations whose rights, liberties, and lives are sacrificed to our reliance for our own safety on the cruelty of foreign dictators.

We will become a particularly despised enemy of those mistakenly identified as terrorists or abused by their government for purely political opposition. To the extent we appear responsible for severe violations of human rights, we will also face the storm of domestic opposition that caused France to leave Algeria and the United Kingdom and the United States to divide over British handling of Northern Ireland.

These are difficult questions. But there is no avoiding the fact that we have to take seriously the tradeoff between the safety of Americans and the liberty of those abroad in the face of regimes doing, or pretending to do, our bidding. As long as others believe that the American people would willingly buy a small amount of increased safety in exchange for the torture, detention, or imprisonment of many innocents abroad, we cannot sustain any claim to moral leadership. And moral leadership has served us well for decades by eliciting popular support in nations around the world—i.e., in terms of freely given support for the policies of the United States.

The Opposing Case

There is, of course, an alternative view of the needs for, and mechanisms of, world leadership. Many in the Bush administration frankly adopt it. It underlies the administration's new national security policy.[12]

As to our needs, the opposing argument goes that we lose more than we gain from international agreements and international institutions. The world's only superpower and supereconomy, it is said, can accomplish more of what it wants by threats and promises than by embodying shared purposes in treaties and organizations. I have argued that threats and promises can reach only as far as the appearance of compliance; and the gap between the gains from that and the benefits of won, and therefore unfeigned, agreement is large. The opposing case emphasizes instead the number of occasions on which we will have to pay in the form of restraining our vast powers for the questionable benefits from others agreeing to something we want.

The rejection by the United States of the International Criminal Court (ICC) is a clear example. We are plainly deeply opposed to genocide, grievous war crimes, and crimes against humanity. We also oppose "aggression," which will be added in the future to the above three areas of jurisdiction. But the opinions of its prosecutors and judges will necessarily fill in many of the gaps in international criminal law in areas where we now can decide for ourselves what is or is not permitted in our worldwide exercises of military force. The meaning of "aggression" is much disputed. The Bush administration does not want international judges shaping domestic and world opinion in ways that will reduce our flexibility of action, let alone punishing our leaders.

More fundamental are differences about the mechanisms of world leadership. Some would argue that I have vastly under-estimated the effect on willing compliance by other nations of a constant show of U.S. power, at least when accompanied by our best explanations of why (and honest belief that) what we are demanding is in the best interests of the world and not just of the United States. A dramatic illustration is the recently released transcript of Che Guevara's comments on the effect on Latin American revolutionaries of U.S. threats leading to the removal of Soviet missiles from Cuba in 1962.

Many Communists. . . are dismayed by the actions of the Soviet Union. A number of divisions have broken up. New groups are springing up, factions are springing up. The thing is, we are deeply convinced of the possibility of seizing power in a number of Latin American countries . . . . But the Soviets' withdrawal means that we can now expect the decline of the revolutionary movements in Latin America . . . . It may cause difficulties for maintaining the unity of the socialist countries. It seems to me there are already cracks in the unity of the socialist camp.[13]

In analogy to an older conflict, some might also argue and hope that we can convince enough of the world that what it needs now is the wisdom of a benevolent superpower, not the self-interest of an oligarchy of first-world nations, and cer-tainly not a plebiscite of self-interested states vastly different in size, power, wealth, virtue, and legitimacy.

That is possible but too unlikely to be the basis of U.S. hopes for world leadership. It is a new message for the United States to bear, and probably an unsaleable one. It is also an unneces-sary message of triumphant unilateralism. Going our own way is always available to us when the inhibitions or costs of a particular treaty or organizational arrangement plainly exceed the benefits and when the advantage of encouraging a regime of treaties does not offset that net loss. The cost of gambling on others' admiration of our success is to encourage others' desires to organize to diminish our role and pretensions. There is too little to gain from proclaiming our independence of the world to make worthwhile that proud announcement.

Part IV

Organizing for the
Necessary Decisions

Chapter 7

The Problem of Drifting into an "Intelligence State"

The center of attention in terms of our long-term capacity to deal with an enduring threat of terrorism has been on the creation of a new Department of Homeland Security. That organization, it is hoped, will sharply increase the focus and cooperation of the organizations responsible for responding to the damage done by terrorist attacks. It will also, it is hoped, improve substantially the coordination of efforts to protect U.S. targets and borders and play a role in managing and supplementing the analytic efforts of our intelligence agencies to anticipate terrorist attacks. But there is much reason to doubt that the new department will solve our most serious problems in addressing terrorism.

Skeptics point out that most business mergers fail, that the price of this reorganization is likely to include huge demands on the time of Secretary Tom Ridge simply to integrate independent units, and that this expenditure of energy will be a distraction from the task of identifying national needs and inventive solutions.[1] They also note that the new secretary has not been given the power to control the various counter-terrorist activities that have become central responsibilities of the secretary of defense, the director of the Central Intelligence Agency, the secretary of state, the attorney general, and the director of the Federal Bureau of Investigation. Therefore, a high-level White House adviser will still be needed to coordinate *all* efforts, as well as to go beyond coordination: to assure that there are the dedication and resources for whatever is new and promising and not in the repertoire of any of the agencies now handling terrorism.

Moreover, focus on the important responsibilities of the new department other than intelligence is something of a distraction from the attention urgently demanded for improved intelligence handling by those other organizations still responsible for it. In September 2002, a full year after the September 11 attacks, the inspector general of the Department of Justice still found as follows:

The FBI has never performed a comprehensive written assessment of the risk of the terrorist threat facing the United States. Such an assessment would be useful not only to define the nature, likelihood, and severity of the threat but also to identify intelligence gaps that needed to be addressed. Moreover, we believe that comprehensive threat and risk assessments would be useful in determining where to allocate attention and resources—both within the FBI and government-wide—on programs and initiatives to combat terrorism.[2]

Moreover,

[the FBI had no formal] assessments of the training, skill level, resources, sophistication, specific capabilities, intent, likelihood of attack, and potential targets of terrorist groups. Further, the draft report does not discuss the methods that terrorists might use. For example, there is no analysis of terrorists' progress toward developing or acquiring chemical, biological, radiological, and nuclear weapons or any discussion of what the FBI has learned from its past terrorist investigations.[3]

For these reasons, many have recommended a shift in the allocation of responsibilities for domestic intelligence. A distinguished panel assembled by the Markle Foundation produced a persuasive argument that, while the FBI should continue to gather secret domestic intelligence, the Department of Homeland Security should determine what was needed, combine it with other intelligence, analyze the results, and see to their distribution.[4] More dramatically, Senator John Edwards of North Carolina offered legislation creating a new domestic intelligence agency to replace the FBI in this field.[5]

These are obviously major management challenges still to be addressed by Congress, the president, and the agency heads. But there is a policy issue as great and as demanding as the management problems that may divert our attention. The perceived importance of the intelligence component may herald serious risks to democratic freedoms. Thus, what is of equal moment but has not been considered is the risk that—in the course of creating new organizations, distributing resources, and granting new powers—we may end up creating an "intelligence state," very different from the United States we have had during peacetime for more than two centuries.

In the long run, the focus of our efforts is going to be intelligence—gathering it at home and abroad, effectively combining what different agencies and different countries gather, and creatively imagining what the full picture looks like. By 2003, there had already been major shifts of resources and manpower to counterterrorism intelligence in France, Britain, and the United States.[6] Much of the world, particularly in Eastern Europe and the Middle East, has experienced "intelligence states" where information about citizens is gathered extremely broadly, and the activities of intelligence agencies are unconstrained. As a result, fear of the government and suspicion of one's neighbors is widespread; and open political opposition wanes as do the institutions of civil society. We are not likely to proceed to the end of that road, but we have to worry about traveling even part way. A central issue is thus how to gather intelligence effectively and, at the same time, avoid becoming an "intelligence state."

A Future to Be Feared

Imagine it is the year 2010. Fear of terrorism could have changed our society in all of the following ways. The government might be making more significant efforts to track the movement and activities of all Americans, keeping more extensive files and using the military to do this. During the Vietnam War the army's collection of files on citizen activities included "files on the membership, ideology, programs, and practices of virtually every activist group in the country. These included not only violence-prone organizations ... but such non-violent groups as the Southern Christian Leadership Conference, Clergy and Laymen United Against the War in Vietnam, the American Civil Liberties Union, Women Strike for Peace, and the National Association for the Advancement of Colored People."[7] Moreover, our intelligence agencies abroad are authorized to turn to disruptive activities ("covert actions") in carrying out their roles. That model led the FBI to its COINTELPRO[8] program of secret disruption of groups and slander of individuals in the United States at the time of the Vietnam War.

To help keep track of citizen activities, the government in 2010 could encourage citizens to report even remote suspicions about their neighbors, and it could place informants in religious groups and political groups sympathetic to organizations the government found either dangerous or critical of the vigor of the government's effort to deal with terrorism. It could use electronic surveillance and secret physical searches far more freely and frequently, perhaps with statutory changes to facilitate this.

The president might well assert much more expansively the claimed military power to detain Americans or aliens indefinitely when the government suspected someone of relations with international terrorists, and continue refusing to account for the number or names of people detained. It could isolate the individuals detained from family and attorneys for prolonged interrogation.

The government could regularly exercise the claimed power to try long-time residents, perhaps including citizens, before closed military tribunals if it suspected them of terrorism. In these activities, it could claim that secrecy precluded being accountable to Congress or to the courts.

Abroad, the government might by 2010 have come to routinely use the services of torturers and murderers to further our intelligence or safety, accepting the CIA's claim that even requiring higher-level approval of such agents created dangerous inhibitions among our intelligence officers. It might engage abroad in kidnapping or assassination of those foreigners the government suspected had terrorist ties.

All of these steps have real precedents, either during the Vietnam War, as in the case of extensive military spying on citizens, or as experiments or announced possibilities in the period since September 11. Less foreshadowed by current events are other facets of an intelligence state: threatening punishment if citizens do not report suspicious activities; or denying access to certain places, at least to Muslims or to those with an Arab background or others whose beliefs or ethnicity suggest a greater-than-average relation to a terrorist group.

At the furthest extreme, we might find this future American government taking a path Israel and the United Kingdom took and engaging in torture or inhumane treatment at home in situations where intelligence officials conclude (and perhaps persuade a judge) that a terrorist attack is imminent, and that the person tortured may have information that could prevent it. More likely, the absence of exclusionary rules would encourage the use of extremely prolonged interrogation in the absence of a lawyer or friend, with the assumption that the results would not be used in trial. Perhaps frustration could even lead us—as it has other Western democracies—to adopt forms of deterrent punishment of the families of terrorists who seem otherwise to be either unlocatable or undeterrable themselves.

The objectives of this wider range of activities would not be corralled, as criminal investigation is, by relevance to a particular criminal charge. If by 2010 we had chosen an "intelligence state," there would be a far wider interest in any actions which, in the words of the British Security Service Act of 1989, are "intended to overthrow or undermine . . . democracy by political, industrial, or violent means." As a particular instance, political memberships and political speech, which are now generally unavailable as the subjects of prosecution and thus criminal investigation in the United States, would be important sources of intelligence about those likely to commit dangerous acts. The scope of intelligence-gathering would be as broad as the presidential sense of "danger" or "extreme danger." Vast quantities of information about wholly innocent activities would be collected by intelligence agencies in the hope that they "may" tie into something else later. Indeed, there is a substantial amount of social control that comes from simply conveying the notion that everyone and everything is being watched.[9]

In short, a state that relies on intelligence activities instead of criminal investigations is likely to look promising as a more effective way of preventing terrorism, but it would create grave new risks. Intelligence agencies can define the threats they address, are not limited by definitions of crimes, are not limited in gathering private information to what is more than suggestive, have no burden of establishing the reliability of their product beyond a reasonable doubt, can engage in illegal activities secretly, and thus without political accountability, and can readily be turned to political purposes or allowed to drift in that direction. All these are the costs that come with the important benefits of special skills and a culture of prevention through anticipation of attacks. Nor have these powers and roles proved temporary in other countries—terminating with the threat that justified them. Intelligence agencies around the world have stretched to find new ways to serve their political masters when old needs and former demands have been satisfied.

Justified by public fears of dangerous organizations that are visible only to the intelligence agencies, often focused on a group or activity that most of the population does not identify with and thus avoiding threatening the majority, intelligence agencies can be as strong as the national fears they help define. Moreover, for at least three reasons the steps they take when the fears are greatest have the tendency to endure. They become precedents for later arguments. They encourage suspicion of unseen, treacherous enemies that intimidate organized opposition. Over time, caution about dissent becomes an accepted social custom and a habitual individual reaction. The fear of such drifts was one of the important motivations for our national Bill of Rights.

Building Intelligence Capacities without Creating an "Intelligence State"

The good news is that the United States has learned a great deal about how to control intelligence agencies without paying a significant price in the amount of information gathered. What we learned from intelligence excesses in the decade prior to 1975 is now embodied in four critically important protections that have served us well. The risk is only that failure to remember what we have learned by hard experience can lead us to an intelligence state.

1. KEEP INTERNAL SECURITY FUNCTIONS OUT OF THE HANDS OF THE MILITARY AND THE CIA

There is room for serious debate about whether our domestic intelligence would be better handled by a separate internal intelligence agency, such as operates in almost every Western democracy except ours, or by continuing our tradition of having intelligence functions carried out by the Federal Bureau of Investigation, which also has criminal responsibilities. Since the functions are somewhat different—one being reactive and one being preventive—the needed skills may be different. That would suggest a separate intelligence agency. On the other hand, there are very substantial advantages in terms of lawfulness with the present arrangement where FBI agents move, with successive assignments, between the familiar duties to law and courts of criminal investigators, and the methods and duties of intelligence-gathering. The agents develop instincts of lawfulness that can help maintain legality, even when they have shifted to an intelligence capacity, where the activities are largely secret. Moreover, agents can be quickly and conveniently shifted back to law enforcement duties when there are not demanding intelligence responsibilities.

Whatever the resolution of this issue, it is critical that domestic and foreign intelligence remain the responsibilities of separate agencies. Agencies gathering foreign intelligence are given far greater freedom than those dealing with their own citizens. CIA officers operating abroad are not generally subject to our criminal law. They are often expected to violate the laws of the states where they are operating. They are not bound by the prohibitions of customary international laws; treaties are binding but rarely applicable to intelligence activities.

Within the United States, we want a very different attitude toward the law. That is one of the reasons that most Western democracies have domestic intelligence agencies that are distinct from their foreign intelligence agencies, even if, unlike the United States, they utilize for domestic intelligence specialized agents with no relation to the culture of criminal law enforcement and legality.

It is at least equally important to limit the powers of the military to gather intelligence within our borders. Fear of the military is a general characteristic of many nations, but not the United States, where popular approval of the institution is usually very high. This approval reflects the steps, starting with the second and third amendments to our Bill of Rights, that we have taken to eliminate the fear. In 1792, the Congress passed a statute that limited the president's ability to use military force to restore order. Repealed at the beginning of the

Civil War, such legislation reappeared in 1878 with the *Posse Comitatus Act*,[10] which denied the military the right to "execute the law," except in cases of civil disorder, insurrection, or rebellion.

That statute—which has remained in effect for more than 120 years, although with additional exceptions—allows the military to act at home only to repress "unlawful obstructions, combinations, or assemblages, or rebellions against the United States," that make it "impracticable to enforce the laws of the United States . . . by the ordinary course of judicial proceedings" (10 U.S.C.§§ 331 and 332). The president may also use the military when citizens are deprived of their constitutional rights by domestic violence or insurrection and state authorities cannot remedy the situation. Technical or logistical assistance to law enforcement agencies is also permitted.

Broadly denied the right or responsibility to engage in law enforcement in the absence of insurrection or massive civil disorder, the military has generally not been feared at home. At the same time, the territorial restrictions on its responsibilities have meant that it has had no need to gather intelligence about domestic activities to carry out its operations.

The exceptions to this tradition in the United States have been inglorious, undermining the vast store of public confidence in the military. During World War I, army intelligence worked with the American Protective League, an organization of civilians volunteering to investigate disloyalty, that established a wide network of informants who "reported to the army not only on suspected German spies and sympathizers, but also on labor unions, socialists, communists, aliens, and even U.S. Attorneys who, in their opinions, lacked sufficient anti-German fervor."[11]

Military internal security activities blossomed again with the domestic disturbances caused by the civil rights movement, the anti-Vietnam War movement, and the urban riots in the late 1960s. Military intelligence gathered information indiscriminately about perfectly peaceful organizations. Military agents infiltrated civilian organizations, sitting among delegates on the floor of the 1968 Republican National Convention, posing as press photographers and newsmen, joining the poor people's campaign, posing as students to monitor classes in the black studies program at New York University, and becoming part of a coalition of church youth groups. The results were files kept on a large number of individuals, including their financial affairs, sex lives, and psychiatric histories.[12] Although statutory proposals to prohibit such activities failed to pass, they were stopped administratively after exposure by the Church Committee hearings in the Senate in the 1970s, leaving the FBI our only federal agency with internal security responsibilities.

An administration without a sense of history or without concern for the risks could, of course, secretly change this exclusion of the CIA and the military from domestic intelligence-gathering. Indeed, there are some costs to the exclusion of the military and the CIA. They have resources that may be underutilized. If so, there is a cost of duplication in producing the same capabilities in the FBI or an independent domestic intelligence agency. Perhaps more salient in light of the failures that led up to September 11, insisting on separating intelligence-gathering activities at home from those abroad creates problems in combining the information gathered in the United States with the information that is gathered abroad. The benefits are, however, well worth the cost, even if we were only counting the risks to national support for the Defense Department and the CIA, let alone if we include serious concerns about democratic freedoms.

2. DEFINE THE PERMISSIBLE SCOPE OF DOMESTIC INTELLIGENCE

At about the time of the Church Committee hearings, Attorney General Levy responded to fears of FBI abuse of internal security investigations by promulgating guidelines for domestic intelligence-gathering. If a group and not a crime were to be investigated, unless the group worked for a foreign state or party, the FBI had to have a reasonable suspicion that it was involved in planning criminal violence. The Privacy Act made the keeping of files dependent on the proper opening of an investigation; so files could not be kept unless there was a reason to believe the organization was actively planning criminal violence. Different rules applied to the opening of investigations on individuals who were agents of foreign states or parties (such as Al Qaeda). A reasonable belief as to that status, when combined with reason to suspect the group of terrorist activities, warranted an investigation of the organization and keeping files on what was found.

These rules impose a far more restrictive definition of the permissible areas of domestic intelligence-gathering than the requirements of most Western nations. That is important, but what is crucial is that the subjects of permissible intelligence-gathering be carefully and publicly defined. Government information-gathering about citizens creates an intimidating power. Secret intelligence activity at home—because it generally gathers information about matters the individual has tried to keep private and also because secrecy creates unaccountability for additional (i.e., not information-gathering) actions against an individual—is particularly intimidating.

Governments gather and store information in a variety of ways, secret and open, for a variety of purposes. These are reflected in Figure 7.1.

The rows A–E on Figure 7.1 represent the major occasions for governmental information-gathering, processing, storage, and analysis. Governments need to gather information for purposes of foreign policy and defense; for the control or punishment of crime; to prevent certain grave dangers, including prominently guaranteeing the safety of the president and other government leaders; and to inform domestic policy, such as making wise political appointments. Since the most powerful leaders in a democracy are elected, they often want infor-

In What, If Any, Circumstances:

	1. Can you use special powers to gather information, generally secretly?	2. Can you use agencies specializing in secret information-gathering or covert operations?	3. Can you use covert operations to influence groups, parties, and states?	4. Can you make and keep files on individuals?	5. Can you use a centralized information compiling and analysis unit?	6. Should you not use governmental agencies or funds at all?
A. Foreign policy and defense						
B. To gather evidence needed to bring a prosecution						
C. To prevent grave dangers (including threats to president or foreign heads of state)						
D. To aid routine government decision-making (including presidential appointments)						
E. For political or personal purposes						

Needs and Purposes Justifying Information-gathering

Figure 7.1 Powers of Government Agencies Whose Primary Function Is Information-gathering and Processing (cells might, for example, be filled in with: "always," "never," or "only under carefully specified circumstances")

mation for political purposes (or even for personal use). Hardly an accepted justification for intelligence-gathering, political or personal use becomes possible because of the secrecy surrounding intelligence-gathering and use.

Purposes must be matched with permitted or forbidden intelligence activities. No one expects a government to refrain from gathering and using generally available public information. The question about government powers arises with regard to the *secret* gathering of private information or its collection and analysis, as well as with regard to secret actions taken to confuse, bribe, extort, or threaten individuals in a way that cannot be readily traced to the government. The column headings in Figure 7.1 reflect the variety of these special powers.

The activities in the first row pose little threat to the personal security of citizens or the strength of democracy, as they deal primarily with information about people, organizations, and events abroad. The fact that U.S. agencies gathering foreign intelligence—such as the Central Intelligence Agency (CIA) or the National Security Agency (NSA)—have been created (see column 2) and vested with special powers (see column 1), including the authority to use covert operations to influence groups, parties, and states abroad (see column 3), is rarely a threat to citizens. Nor is it a threat to citizens that the special powers go far beyond the ability to reach otherwise unavailable sights and sounds through satellites and spy planes and include the ability to process, combine, and compare items of information in ways that are far beyond the means of ordinary citizens. It is not a threat to democracy or to the citizen's civil liberties that the nation's intelligence agencies, working abroad, can maintain and analyze files on foreign individuals and organizations (see columns 4 and 5). This is plainly an appropriate use of governmental powers and resources (see column 6).

The critical matter for information-gathering for the purpose of foreign policy and defense is that it excludes powers to investigate or disrupt the activities of citizens so long as they are not working on behalf of a foreign government. The following rows focus on information-gathering or actions taken within the country and affecting citizens: the use of governmental powers and specialized agencies to gather information or disrupt for political or personal purposes or to create, store, and analyze files for political or personal reasons (see row E) can be no more appropriate, and is far more dangerous, than the use of governmental cars or buildings for the same purposes.

The contested areas of governmental information-gathering in a democracy are represented by rows B, C, and D: law enforcement, preventing grave dangers, and informing domestic policy. In these three areas, some information-gathering is obviously an appropriate activity for governmental agencies (see column 6). The questions in these areas are related to what special powers and secret information-gathering organizations should be permitted; what, if any, covert operations to influence groups or individuals should be allowed; and what collection of information that could be used in the exercise of governmental discretion should be permitted.

The need for information to support policymaking (see row D) has generally not led to a claim of special powers to gather information and to keep files on individuals. The scope of the special investigative powers granted in the case of law enforcement (see row B)—the investigative powers of government including the use of informants, governmental agents, and electronic surveillance—has been the subject of historic and open debate in the United States. The use by the CIA of covert actions abroad to influence groups and states (see column 3) led in the 1960s to the FBI undertaking a similar program within the United States. This in turn led to a public reaction so severe as to broadly discourage such activity when only American citizens are involved, whether the justification is crime control or internal security.[13]

The most troublesome aspect of information-gathering is related to the prevention of grave dangers (see row C), because it invites the use of exceptional powers (a) against citizens within the country and (b) without necessarily having, as a basis, statutory crimes (which would limit the reach of the intrusion and the ultimate purpose of the actions of the information-gathering agency). The justifications for this are that sometimes prevention is much more important than prosecution and that the information required may go beyond that needed to convict. Professor Peter Russell of the University of Toronto, for example, describes Canada's worst intelligence lapse as the failure to discover the Sikh effort to blow up an Air India plane, which resulted in hundreds of deaths. Preventing that bombing would have required unusually broad and intrusive surveillance. The argument is that prevention of grave dangers may justify two departures from ordinary rules of criminal justice: *availability of special investigative powers in a broader range of situations* (not just to obtain evidence of crimes) and *wider and more lasting investigations.*

Of course, an occasion of secret intelligence-gathering may appear to protesters or dissenters to be political in nature or an effort to repress dissent, and yet appear to its supporters as an effort to prevent a grave danger. Unless there are substantial efforts to be clear, the lines separating mere opposition or permissible dissent in politics from a real internal danger are likely to be crossed by whoever controls intelligence capacities. It is therefore critical to define a very clear line to quiet public insecurity and the fears held by political opponents. The possible subjects for internal security investigations related to preventing "grave dangers" must be carefully limited or citizens will fear they are always subject to investigation or some sort of covert operation or worse, at least whenever the members of an internal security agency could associate them with rejection of the main political parties.

Drawing on international practice, it is possible to identify five ways to limit the otherwise awesome scope of secret powers granted to prevent "grave dangers."

1. The narrowest possibility is to forbid non-criminal internal investigations completely. Knowingly planning something that would be a grave danger to the population or the state is almost always a crime. So, it is reasonable and possible to say that there should be no special powers—that criminal investigative powers are sufficient.

The United States comes close to this with regard to cases that have no foreign component, requiring evidence of a planned violent crime before anyone can open an investigation into domestic terrorism (or organized crime). Canada rejected this option as too narrow, including within its mandate to the Canadian security intelligence service:

Activities directed toward undermining by covert unlawful acts, or directed toward or intended ultimately to lead to the destruction or overthrow by violence of, the constitutionally established system of government in Canada.

2. The next narrowest category of secret information-gathering justified by internal threats would include only the power to investigate threats to the president, or representatives of foreign governments and parties, or political and popular leaders. Like the United States, many nations have a special agency—in the United States, the Secret Service—whose intelligence responsibility is solely in this category. Under this category would also fall preventive investigation in cases of international events that are likely to elicit some form of violent attack, such as the Olympics, or a meeting of the International Monetary Fund. It is difficult to imagine not granting special investigative powers here.

3. The next narrowest scope would add to this, as a basis for granting special powers for internal security investigations, situations involving a danger traceable to a foreign source. The Foreign Intelligence Surveillance Act in the United States grants special powers to wiretap and search in cases of espionage and terrorism which have a significant foreign component. Canada includes matters of international meddling by covert opera-

tions. Intended to guarantee the security of its citizens against secret activities by foreign agents, the Canadian policy allows special investigations of any dangerous or disruptive activities traceable to foreign states or foreign powers.

4. Equally compelling as a ground for internal security jurisdiction, and adopted by many Western democracies, is permission for an internal security agency to investigate all cases of severe, politically motivated, danger to the people or the Constitution. Everywhere this includes the threat of violent terrorism or violent domestic disturbance. The critical distinction within this category is whether either planned and imminent violence or foreign connections should be required, as it is in the United States, or whether, as in Germany, Britain, and Canada, a domestic plan to overthrow the constitutional structure by a broader, even non-violent, set of unlawful means and at some undetermined future date is adequate.

5. The broadest jurisdiction has been occasioned by the collapse of the Soviet Union. The foreign intelligence agencies in the non-communist world then found themselves with capacities for information-gathering far in excess of the well-established targets within the Soviet Empire. Led by the CIA, intelligence agencies took on at least part of the responsibility for gathering information to address problems of well-organized crime involving drugs, sale of weapons, transfer of critical technology, etc.

In the United States, this jurisdiction was added only to the responsibilities of agencies working abroad gathering foreign intelligence. In other countries, often where there was a unified responsibility for foreign and internal intelligence, the new jurisdictions were assigned to internal intelligence agencies. The scope of this, the broadest prevalent extension of jurisdiction over internal security matters, could be limited to forms of well-organized crime that operated on an international basis, but frequently it is not. The unlimited version is, for example, the pattern in South Africa, although there is a continuing argument about whether an internal intelligence agency is needed there at all. When an intelligence agency has powers to gather information on criminal activity, the general pattern is that it must turn this information over to a criminal investigative group, making no use of the information itself.

There are few costs to national security from carefully defining, and making public, the jurisdiction of a domestic intelligence agency. It tells people who believe they are clearly not in the area of permissible jurisdiction that they will not be investigated, but that is precisely what we want to happen in order to free their activities from a burden of fear. The definition may inadvertently exclude activities that become sources of severe danger at a later date, but there can easily be provision for investigation for a limited period of time, pending amendment. Once again, the benefits seem well worth the cost.

3. LIMIT THE INTELLIGENCE AGENCY TO STATUTORILY DEFINED LEGAL POWERS

In many Western democracies, powers of the domestic intelligence agency have been undefined, much as the powers of foreign intelligence agencies, such as the CIA, are not defined by statute. The officers of the agency are expected, but not legally empowered, to engage in activities that would be criminal for private citizens. With that form of dilemma in mind, President Reagan pardoned two of the most senior officials of the FBI for breaking into homes looking for evidence about the politically violent Weathermen. A highly admired CIA director, Richard Helms, pled guilty to lying under oath to a congressional committee while his famous lawyer called the conviction a "badge of honor." In each case, there was considerable ambiguity as to whether normal laws applied to actions by intelligence officials within the United States. Ending that ambiguity is important in itself.[14]

The truly grave danger is, of course, to those whose civil and criminal rights are subject to violation by a government-funded, powerful agency whose activities have not been authorized by the legislature. President Nixon used a special unit, "the Plumbers," to break into private locations for largely political purposes. The way to prevent this, too, is to require domestic intelligence agencies to use only those powers they have been accorded by statute.

That is, in fact, the way the United States has operated since the mid-1970s. Searches and electronic surveillance can be conducted under different standards when the purpose is intelligence-gathering. But the standards have, over much resistance of the executive branch, been set forth legislatively and publicly in the Foreign Intelligence Surveillance Act.[15] That statute has been used more than 14,000 times. It has worked admirably both in enabling intelligence officials to investigate foreign spies and terrorists and in assuring the public that there are only limited, specified circumstances in which the government may use secret, intrusive investigative techniques.

The absence of any statutory power to interfere with or disrupt the activities of a group believed to be engaged in domestic violence has been understood to mean that the FBI lacks that authority. It has not claimed that power since the 1970s. The absence of any special authorization to arrest for purposes of prevention or interrogation should carry the same message, although President Bush and Defense Secretary Rumsfeld have asserted that power.

There is no cost to offset these benefits of requiring legislative authorization of the secret activities of an intelligence agency—activities which are also not authorized by any court. We know that the Foreign Intelligence Surveillance Act has worked, and worked well. If specific additional powers are needed, they can and should be legislated by a very willing Congress. If broad additional powers are needed to deal with ongoing national emergencies, they too can be legislated and limited to circumstances that are at least defined generally.

4. THE CRITICAL IMPORTANCE OF OVERSIGHT

Domestic intelligence agencies must act in secret. If what they do is known to terrorists or spies, they will not be able to gather information needed to prevent political violence and espionage. But allowing government activities to be secret, unless they are carefully guarded by oversight, means that rules and limits on jurisdiction and responsibility are likely to be ignored. Officials obey rules either because of personal or organizational sanctions, or because they agree with the principles behind them. If all the capabilities of a large and well-funded organization are dedicated to maintaining the secrecy of its activities, familiar sanctions cannot be relied upon. If the agency has embedded in its culture a belief that national security concerns, as it defines them, trump more "remote" worries about domestic freedoms, particularly the concerns of groups that are not themselves being investigated, rules will lack moral force as well.

Enforcement of rules protecting democratic liberties and assuring an adequate measure of effectiveness and efficiency in gathering and processing intelligence depends upon creating an oversight agency that has the following capacities: knowing what the intelligence agency is doing; having the power to deter the agency from either illegal activities or ineffective, sloppy intelligence-gathering; and the willingness and incentives of whoever has that power and that knowledge to encourage effective, law-abiding behavior.[16] Consider these one at a time.

The central problem of designing an oversight body with full knowledge of intelligence activities, yet a very apparent willingness to insist on discipline and lawfulness, is that the needed strictness and discipline often requires an obviously independent *outside* oversight body while full knowledge and frankness requires an oversight body more closely connected to those responsible for intelligence-gathering (who must be able to rely confidently on the discretion of the oversight body). In general, we confide in people we know to be loyal to us. But if the public is to have confidence in oversight and if oversight is to be effective, the oversight body must not be loyal to, subservient to, or easily deceived by, the intelligence agency.

More specifically, getting intelligence agencies to willingly provide the information needed by an oversight body to broadly monitor intelligence activity depends on providing a very high measure of assurance that a body whose independence the public can trust will not make secret information public in the course of receiving secret reports, calling hearings, and inquiring about complaints.

The resolution of this dilemma, in most Western democracies, is to create an independent or legislative body whose purposes are generally shared with the intelligence agencies and thus can be expected to protect national security secrets, but is independent enough to, at the same time, enjoy public trust. To get these characteristics simultaneously, the oversight bodies in other nations have generally been composed in one of three ways: (1) some of its members are from other political parties than the administration; (2) the oversight body consists of legislators or political opponents who see themselves as likely to be among the first threatened by an uncontrolled intelligence agency; or (3) the members of the oversight body are of great national reputation for integrity or are officials (often judicial) whose positions somehow guarantee that integrity. Arrangements for congressional oversight in the United States utilize all three.

Any of a number of variations of legislative bodies and appointed commissions can satisfy these conditions fairly well, as has been demonstrated in the United States, the United Kingdom, the Netherlands, South Africa, and Germany. However, one additional condition must be satisfied. Whatever the structure of the oversight body, the credibility of the effort—the assurance that the body will not be deceived by the intelligence agencies—depends on the availability to it of adequately trained staff. A body with inadequately trained staff cannot possibly provide the needed oversight.

The oversight body must also have both the power and the will to deter, or to trigger sanctions by others against, violations of law or failures of performance that are known. The first is the easier to provide. The power of U.S. intelligence oversight committees to deter depends on one of three conditions: access to budget authority; authority to remove agency leaders from their positions; or agency fear of adverse publicity and public resentment generated by hearings. (The latter is a difficult sanction to use while preserving secrecy.) It is worth noting that in no country—not even in the United States—is the threat of criminal prosecution real enough to deter violations of democratic liberties by agencies acting in the name of national security.

Finally, effective outside oversight depends on the oversight body's willingness to use its knowledge and its powers to enforce professionalism and respect for democratic liberties. Bodies responsible for auditing the expenditure of government funds (some of whose members have been granted the needed security clearances) are likely to have the motivation needed where misuse of funds is involved, but, because of the financial focus, cannot be the only source of outside oversight. The other motivation can come either from personal commitment, strong enough to overcome any temptations or threats offered by, or loyalty to, the intelligence agency, or from responsiveness to public demands for strong remedial action. For the latter, steps must be taken to nourish public interest in lawfulness and professionalism in intelligence agencies. The two go together, for many people are just as concerned about the effectiveness of intelligence agencies as for the agency's respect for democratic values.

Internal oversight can usefully supplement an outside oversight agency. Redundancy increases the probability that information will be reliably furnished to all of the oversight agencies (because it is likely to be learned by one or another of them). Internal oversight also allows the executive to be as well informed as the outside bodies to which they are accountable. This can take any number of forms. The United States and many other nations utilize an internal inspector general to whom either the agency head or the outside oversight body can assign responsibility for gathering particular information about intelligence activity and reporting on effectiveness and lawfulness. The sharply critical report of the inspector general of the Department of Justice on the detention of hundreds of illegal aliens after September 11 is a bold example. The inspector generals for the CIA and the FBI in the United States are cleared for the highest intelligence information, and are entitled to obtain all information and files that they consider necessary for an investigation. Their reports, which go both to the agency head and, if requested, to the oversight committees of the Congress, are generally classified, although they may also furnish an unclassified version.

For obvious reasons, accountability to an informed public is less promising. Intelligence cannot be a transparent business. The Freedom of Information Act, which was passed in 1966, provides citizens with information in the hands of executive agencies, including those dealing with national security. But it is severely limited in the area of intelligence, as it must be if sources and methods of intelligence-gathering are to be protected. The act has exceptions for matters that are properly classified under an executive order, and those which could reasonably be expected to disclose intelligence sources and methods. Although these determinations are subject to *de novo* judicial review, such review has always reflected great deference to the executive branch in the area of national security.

In the period since September 11, the intelligence committees have complained frequently of the difficulty of getting full information from the FBI and the CIA. Without that cooperation, it is extremely unlikely that even congressional overseers can reliably discover what is or is not being done by an intelligence agency. The 1998 Intelligence Oversight Act thus requires the intelligence agencies to keep the House and Senate Intelligence committees fully and currently informed of all intelligence activities and to "furnish any information or material concerning intelligence . . . which is requested by either of the Intelligence Committees." Any failure to comply with the obligation on the grounds that the Intelligence committees cannot be trusted to maintain secrecy about proper intelligence activities defies the overwhelming experience of the last decade and a half.

In this case, too, there is no adequate argument for avoiding the very carefully designed oversight that is essential to the public sense of confidence, and to any real assurance that the jurisdictional understandings and rules about activities which guide our domestic intelligence are taken seriously.

Conclusion

If the core of American efforts to deal with the danger of terrorism after September 11 is in the area of intelligence, we must take very seriously the problems of a state that allows and funds secret intelligence-gathering and storage on a large scale, i.e., an intelligence state. An extrapolation from steps the Bush administration has taken would lead, as one not unlikely possibility, to a society far less free and far less trusting than the one we have lived in for many decades. Avoiding that possibility is the major structural challenge of dealing with terrorism in the years ahead.

Fortunately, we have learned how to control domestic intelligence-gathering in a more reliable way than almost any country. We have institutionalized a separation between domestic and foreign intelligence. We, like almost all Western democracies, have avoided the dangers that emerged in the years after 1960 from the use of the military to conduct domestic intelligence. Not avoiding those dangers has led to tragic consequences in Latin America. And we have learned the importance of defining the areas of legitimate intelligence interests. Our traditional lines are very narrow and have proved adequate since the 1970s. If they are to be changed, the change should be public.

We have learned the value of restricting intelligence agencies to legislatively enacted powers where they are to do anything that, in the case of ordinary citizens, would be a violation of domestic criminal or civil law. Finally, we have created a system of oversight that both protects our secrets and, in a way persuasive to a broad public, guarantees compliance with the law.

We must insist on the maintenance of these four pillars of a policy designed to control the secret activities of well-funded state agencies whose energies are otherwise very much at the disposal of the president. That is the most important structural challenge as we move into an increasing reliance on intelligence-gathering to reduce the danger of terrorism. Maintaining these protections will not threaten our ability to gather intelligence; abandoning them will, in fact, threaten our capacity to maintain an open and vigorous society.

Chapter 8

Values and Security

The task of dealing with the threat of terrorism involves at least four stages: efforts to prevent the terrorist event; crisis management as it is occurring (for example, dealing with hostage situations); managing the consequences of the attack to minimize the damage with effective, coordinated actions by police, firefighters, health personnel, and emergency management teams; and efforts at retaliation or deterrence aimed either at state sponsors, organizations, or individual terrorists. The United States has had considerable experience in dealing with hostage situations, including particularly hijackings, and with retaliation and deterrence. The two great new areas for us are prevention and consequence management. The former has provided the focus of this book because quite simply, the dangers from massive terrorism attacks, however well their consequences are managed, seem greater than they did before September 11—too great to be given second place to any other aspect of the problem.

A review of three steps or stages is important as a conclusion. First, it is worth ending with an overview of the broad setting for our choices. Any choice begins with some orientation. Then, we should review how we can generate a rich list of alternatives without ignoring important possibilities. Finally, it is important not to end without a look at how we can assess what we are doing so that even a well-oriented choice from among many alternatives is subject to critical evaluation in light of the ways being mistaken about the situation or the likely terrorist responses could make our choices wrong.

The Broad Setting for Our Prevention Efforts

My colleague Alan Dershowitz entitled his book on terrorism *Why Terrorism Works.*[1] The historic record is that terrorism rarely wins. It is generally crushed by the immensely more powerful repressive forces of dictatorial states. Military and intelligence cooperation crushed terrorism in a dozen Latin American countries. It has crushed terrorism against the governments of Egypt, Algeria, and a number of other Middle Eastern states, despite government structures that are often corrupt and unpopular. Terrorists based abroad may be more difficult to destroy, but the odds would still favor greatly a power that abandoned moral, legal, and democratic limits.

Torture will loosen tongues; electronic eavesdroppers can overhear conversations; and far closer to 100 percent of the terrorists can be imprisoned or killed if the country is willing to apply that treatment to anyone who "may" be a terrorist than if it insists on "proof beyond a reasonable doubt." Some of that may make Chile's Pinochet or his generals violators of international humanitarian law, but it works in the long run.

So the challenge is not to beat and stop terrorism. The trick is to do it in a way most consistent with the values of a democratic society. The British, Germans, and Italians all set themselves that objective when under terrorist assault at home. It is less dramatic than "war," but it does not leave the state a pariah or the population deeply disillusioned or, if the focus of repression is on only members of a single sizeable group within the state, deeply divided. And it has been done. The alternative of declaring "all out" and uninhibited "war" on "terrorism with a global reach" is costly in terms of our democracy and, more surprisingly, also in terms of the effectiveness of our efforts to stop terrorist attacks.

In the period since September 11, the Bush administration has explored, although often only on a limited and tentative basis, several anti-terrorist techniques whose promise does not warrant their cost in lost values of a democratic society. Without any showing of need, it has claimed the right to try resident aliens in military tribunals if the secretary of defense thinks they are associated with international terrorism.[2] It has secretly detained low probability suspects, sometimes by manipulating immigration practices and sometimes by a raw assertion of executive power, and for more than 600, closed deportation hearings without anything more than a very general explanation of why secrecy was needed.[3] It has threatened to send and has sent terrorist suspects for foreign interrogation to countries where torture is routine.[4] Defense Secretary Rumsfeld has announced planning for the use of the military to assassinate terror suspects abroad.[5] The administration has created a new class of wartime detainees who are being held in Guantanamo for, as far as they can tell, the indefinite future, and yet denied them the status of prisoners of war.[6]

On almost none of these occasions was the prior authorization of the U.S. Congress or any court called upon. Accompanying all this has also been a strategy of preventing, after the fact, the operation of the separation of powers (denying the need for legislative oversight and the right of judicial review). The costs of not trusting the Congress and the courts are grave and unjustified. So are the costs of keeping material of low strategic importance, such as the number of people detained, secret from the public.

Citing these examples exaggerates the number of people affected in any significant way by the measures we have taken to fight terrorism. They are relatively few, and particularly few if you limit the categories to citizens of the United States. Aliens have borne the brunt of these measures. But, stated starkly, the precedents are plainly frightening, and they are largely attributable to the blanketing of our responses to September 11 with the concept of "war."

Repeating and relying on the concept of "war" is also harmful to fighting terrorism. What we face is a very prolonged series of contests with opponents that do not have the powers of a state, or hope to defeat our armies, or destroy our powerful economy, or threaten to occupy our territory—the dangerous characteristics we have traditionally associated with war. More important, designing our plans as if this is a war leads us badly astray. The dangers we face involve several possible forms of attack by several forms of possible organizations, each of which may have any of a rich set of possible motivations and a rich set of possible organizational structures. This wide range of possibilities must be handled in a variety of different ways— with a subtlety that is obscured by the simpler assumptions hiding behind the term "war." Many of the most important ways do not require, and are not advanced by the use of, our awesome military capacities.

Consider these two dimensions one at a time. As to democratic freedoms, if this were really a war of limited duration, the administration could argue that the only real precedent is that whatever the president feels he needs to do can be done but only for the short and grave period that the nation is at war. The administration could refer to the Civil War and World War II as previous occasions when democratic liberties were set aside. It could rely on what Kathleen Sullivan, the dean of Stanford Law School, calls the "black hole" theory of constitutional rights in wartime: that they temporarily disappear. Two thousand years ago the Romans already knew that law does not survive well in time of war.[7]

The problem is that this "war" is not limited in time, focused in hostility, or all-demanding in sacrifice of our moral resources. We do not face the power of foreign nations. Relatively small nations have been able to crush terrorist groups of equal sizes. We do face extremely serious dangers, particularly from weapons of mass destruction, but that threat can and will come from any of a number of directions and will continue for decades to come. Muslim fundamentalist radicals are not the only angry, violent social movement we will see in the years ahead; and globalization of communication, transportation, and finance puts the United States within the "global reach" of terrorists from different groups with various agendas anywhere in the world.

Developing technology and the spread of knowledge will make the acquisition of weapons of mass destruction more and more possible for smaller and smaller groups. Therein lies the gravest long-range danger we face, and it will be with us for a very long time. The "black hole" theory of democratic freedoms simply will not fit. We cannot take the approach that for some short period of war our democratic liberties are "mothballed." Because the danger is enduring, we must develop ways of adjusting that leave much of what we value in place while we deal with a prolonged period of danger from relatively small groups—only some of which will seek or need state support.

Respecting our democratic freedoms will not dangerously limit how we can and must reduce the risks we face. The needed steps to address the danger are straightforward. At home, as well as at our installations abroad, we have to take protective steps to control access to targets and the resources needed to attack them. The enriched uranium and plutonium necessary for atomic weapons and those weapons themselves must, above all else, be monopolized by states and kept from private hands. This requires funding and diplomacy, not war. Access to either privately or governmentally held ingredients for biological and chemical weapons and, particularly, the means of delivering biological weapons must be restricted or denied. This requires new international law, and international law enforcement, not war.

We should use the threat of our military and economic powers to prevent any state from openly supporting terrorists, and we should use improved intelligence capacity, necessarily combined with that of many other nations, to detect, try, and punish terrorists. The effectiveness of our military threats will always be limited by our inability to detect questionable sincerity and false enthusiasm in the claims of some countries about their efforts to eliminate terrorist groups threatening us. So we will need our own intelligence abroad to verify that cooperation and to substitute for foreign cooperation when it is lacking.

Producing extremely effective intelligence at home and abroad requires better gathering of information, better combination of information from different sources, and greater imagination in drawing conclusions from an incomplete set of pieces. In the broadest sense, what we are trying to do with intelligence is to act effectively, but decently, against dangerous groups. Of the ways to do this, the best is to get far better at obtaining and analyzing and handling the information we can legally gather now. Second best is to more freely allow intrusive wiretaps and searches. Worst is to move the goalposts by reducing what has to be proved for detention, or by weakening the procedures for proof by establishing "special courts" or by creating new crimes that require less evidence of intent.

We will need superb domestic (as well as foreign) intelligence agencies to carry out a strategy based so largely on intelligence-gathering at home and abroad, but whatever structure we trust with intelligence-gathering at home must be designed in ways that protect us from becoming even a pale version of an "intelligence state" like East Germany or Guatemala. These states made extensive use of a massive collection of files, demands for information from neighbors and friends, and highly intrusive, broadly targeted eavesdropping. Fortunately, we know how to protect our freedoms as intelligence powers grow. It takes separation of domestic intelligence-gathering from military and foreign intelligence-gathering; a public definition of what are permissible subjects of intelligence-gathering; a restriction of special powers to search or disrupt to those that are granted by the legislature; and, critically, effective oversight. We have to view with deep suspicion abandonment of any one of these four conditions.

Because our intelligence-gathering (as well as efforts to protect our foreign installations) must take place abroad as well as at home, and because the use of military threats to obtain cooperation is too easily avoided by a pretense of cooperation on the part of other countries, we must rely on diplomatic and economic efforts to obtain enthusiastic cooperation across a spectrum of states for action against any terrorists threatening us. The effort is inherently difficult. The history of terrorism is that states guaranteed security by a terrorist group are reluctant to risk that guarantee. So we need an unusual willingness to cooperate and for that we have to show at least that measure of willingness to cooperate that is common among our friends.

The level of cooperation will depend not only on the extent to which the danger is shared and its level, but also on the perceived needs for U.S. support and long-term friendship. There is a danger of a vicious cycle here: the more we sense a hostility to, or disdain for, our plans, the more we will feel we have to rely on our own capacities, to meet our own needs, and not trust our welfare to cooperative international relations. But the more we disparage cooperative relations, the greater the actual hostility we will encounter. Endorsing and obeying international law is an important part of what is required. The president is free, as far as our own courts are concerned, to ignore customary international law, but that has its price; so, too, does an unwillingness to take part in a regime of treaties, or to subject ourselves to new institutions designed to enforce international law.

War and the self-righteousness that accompanies it on all sides hide the critical steps of foreign policy that must be taken, in the long run, to reduce the particular danger that comes with the possibility of our facing very large numbers of hostile individuals and groups from the Arab and broader Muslim world, perhaps with very little in the way of central organization available to, or needed by, them. A very broad swatch of this immense population sees the "war" that we regard as defensive as aggressively threatening control of their "neighborhood." Encouraging such views helps unpopular and undemocratic governments to deflect to the United States the blame for political, economic, and social conditions that generate despair and anger. If the level of terrorism depends, as it may very well, not just on the number of committed terrorists at any one time, but also on the level of resentment of a far broader, supportive population of, for example, Arabs and Muslims, we have to address ourselves to destroying the bridges that terrorists seek to build to some more moderate population. Calling this a "war" (let alone a "crusade") does not help.

There is, of course, an argument that a more reliable way to get cooperation is to maintain and exercise coercive power rather than promising the benefits of shared approaches to the problems of counter-terrorism and development. There is, in fact, good evidence that terrorism was increased by the sense of terrorist victory that accompanied the withdrawal of the United States from Lebanon in 1983 and from Somalia a decade later as well as by the withdrawal of Israel from Lebanon in 2000.[8] If terrorism, like crime, is often the product of the independent actions of large numbers of individuals in small groups, the evidence that a show of power may reduce crime is also worth considering.

Crime seems to have exploded with the end of dictatorial regimes from Moscow to Johannesburg. Many have attributed recent successes in controlling crime in U.S. cities, such as in New York and Boston, to police showing a heightened willingness to crack down on violence. The Bush administration and its national security statements seem to be betting on these mechanisms for winning support in fighting terrorism. But that is too large and concentrated a wager on too untried a path, compared to also winning cooperation in other ways.

In the final analysis, nothing is certain about fighting terrorism and protecting democracy. Events could suddenly change the source, the direction, or the extent of danger. In the meantime we face very serious dangers, particularly from weapons of mass destruction. We can and should dedicate substantial attention and resources to reducing these dangers. But what we cannot do is decide that for the length of time that the danger is with us—perhaps decades—we will abandon the sharing of powers in our own government or our sharing of responsibility with other governments, much less the freedoms of our own citizens.

We must develop ways of adjusting that leave as much as possible of what we value in place. The starting point is to recognize that a very serious continuing danger from weapons of mass destruction is not the equivalent of "war," that most of the steps that must be taken involve cooperative relations with other states in activities from gathering intelligence to preventing weapons of mass destruction from falling into private hands, and that creating either a state of perpetual war or an "intelligence state" will not greatly reduce the danger from such weapons, although it will gravely increase the danger to democracy.

Choosing Actions to Prevent Terrorist Attacks

What we must do to create security in the face of terrorism is not space science. The starting place of any effort to deal with terrorism after September 11 is the development of an adequate array of alternatives. The logic of that is straightforward and set forth in Chapter 3. It goes like this.

Identify the things that terrorists will need to conduct the forms of terrorism that we regard as most dangerous: sustained campaigns, spectacular attacks, or, by far the most serious, the use of nuclear or biological weapons. It is relatively straightforward to make a list of those things. Figure 8.1, first discussed in Chapter 3, captures a first cut in the column headings. The heart of the effort to prevent terrorism is to deny

TERRORIST NEEDS

	A. Recruits and continuing members	B. Resources	C. Training	D. Tactical information	E. Access	F. Means to escape	G. A haven	H. Hope	I. Social acceptance a. by terrorist organization b. by wider support network
1. Reducing enthusiasm for attacks on the United States									
2. Deterrence through law enforcement, military, or economic threats against: a. individuals b. groups c. states									
3. Denying access to: a. targets b. resources c. the United States									
4. Gathering and processing information (intelligence) on individuals, groups, organizations, and activities									
5. Disruption including asset forfeiture and incapacitation through: a. criminal prosecution b. detention									

STATE PREVENTIVE STRATEGIES

Figure 8.1 The Logic of Prevention

the terrorists critical access to as many of these things as possible—at least to deny access to some combination that is critical to their success. We have only five broad categories of ways to accomplish this. Set out as the rows in Figure 8.1, they are described there in quite general terms. The actual list of alternatives would greatly elaborate each of the rows. Some of the alternatives may be illegal (for example, under Row 4 of Figure 8.1, torture for intelligence information is forbidden by U.S. law as well as by international treaties to which we are a signatory). Some may impose significant costs in terms of our democratic freedoms or a sense of the equality of various groups in the population. Some alternatives will have major damaging effects on our foreign relations with friendly countries. Some will prove counter-productive; although they will make more difficult the job of the terrorists in terms of one of the columns of Figure 8.1, at the same time, they will make easier the job under a different column (for example, the effect of assassinations on recruitment and social acceptance). A number of the options require a judgment about a particular situation, at a historical moment. Others require awareness of the long-run benefits of rules and compliance with law.

Having in mind these variations—legality, threats to democratic freedoms, concern about precedent, and counter-productive effects that help the terrorists to meet their other needs—a rich set of alternatives for dealing with any particular type of terrorism at any specific time and place has to be adequately assessed against an adequately rich set of goals. Thinking through the list of more specific possibilities for each broad category of preventive activity can sometimes be done systematically. For example, the denial of access to resources and targets (row 3 of Figure 8.1) requires decisions as to how much risk we are prepared to take for the benefits of more open access. And then we must decide what means of limiting access is to be applied to each of various groups. That is set forth in Figure 8.2.

POSSIBLE BASIS

POSSIBLE ACTIONS	1. Everyone	2. All aliens	3. Temporary visitors	4. Resident aliens an temporary visitors from certain countries	5. Temporary visitors from certain countries	6. Members of, or contributors to (or "associated with") certain political or religious groups with certain ties to terrorism
A. Flatly denying access to all but a few who "need" access						
B. Conditioning access on a relatively full "clearance" investigation						
C. Conditioning access on a review of files, check of documents, or minor investigation						
D. Conditioning access on further checks if there is suspicious activity or a suspicious history						
E. Monitoring access and simply keeping records						
F. No check on access and no monitoring						

Figure 8.2 Alternative Ways of Denying Access to Targets and Resources

Talk of "war" as if that substitutes for a recognition of the complexity of the situation *and* the richness of our goals *and* the variety of our alternatives is simply folly. Let me supply a specific example.

Soon after the attacks of September 11, President Bush announced that he was creating military tribunals that could try resident aliens even for events occurring within the United States. The alternatives we have for disabling an individual who is likely to be planning terrorist attacks (Figure 8.1, Row 5), perhaps in some kind of association with Al Qaeda, include: civilian trial, military trial, detention as an illegal combatant, detention as a POW, detention under presidential order as an illegal combatant, detention for violations of immigration regulations, detention under a new statute passed for that purpose, and assassination. (If the purpose is also to gather information, we have a range of alternatives for that, ranging from more or less coercive interrogation to following the advice of a number of FBI leaders and instead secretly monitoring the individual's activity.)

Presumably advised that in a state of "war" he had the powers both to detain suspects and to subject them to a military tribunal without congressional authority (a quite questionable determination in light of applicable statutes),[9] the president moved immediately to assert those claims of power without assessing the objectives we might be pursuing. If an individual associated with Al Qaeda is active within the United States, we should want to choose the alternative which best serves whichever of the following are our goals:

• To deter future terrorist events;

• To incapacitate a critical mass of those who may engage in planning a terrorist event;

• To gather information about what the plan is and who, if arrested, would prevent execution of the plan;

• *Not* to create new recruits, for example by not creating martyrs;

• *Not* to undermine the support we need from our allies in intelligence and military efforts and in cooperation with our extradition requests;

• *Not* to threaten the feeling of security against abuse by the executive branch that Americans have treasured since 1790; and

• To encourage democratic and decent behavior abroad or, at least, not to make implausible the demand of the United States, as world leader, for civilized behavior.

Depending on a wide variety of factors, one of the other alternatives may be much better than military tribunals in terms of the objectives that concern us most. For example, what we do depends a great deal on whether arresting the suspect is feasible and lawful, the risk of having to reveal secrets, the effects of having a lawyer, the benefits and costs of providing protective procedures before incapacitation or sentence, the political risks of public trial and acquittal, the danger to jurors, and—most important of all—the amount of risk associated with having to meet a high burden of proof, assessed by a truly independent decision-maker. A careful look would have to include consideration of the various possibilities within each of the broad categories of alternatives. For example, we have a powerful statute that has been very effective in protecting our secrets while according a criminal trial.

In fact, there is every reason to believe that our court system can handle a case of anyone arrested in the United States for planning terrorism, at least if the arrest is delayed long enough for investigators to learn what they are seeking to learn about other participants and the nature of the plan; for by then, they will also have enough information to charge and convict for a crime of conspiracy. The basic point was made with reference to civil liberties in Chapter 5 and illustrated in the image reproduced here as Figure 8.3. Military tribunals, for those arrested in the United States, are extremely dangerous to democratic unity and are not needed to reduce the chance and

1. Steps useful to reduce the chance and harms of terrorism

2. Steps dangerous to democratic liberties or national unity

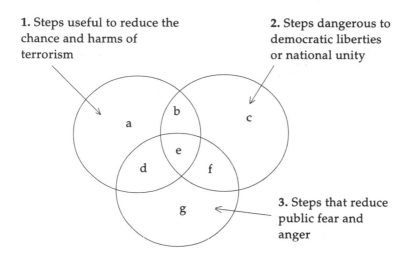

3. Steps that reduce public fear and anger

Figure 8.3 Choice of Actions Incorporating Democratic Freedoms and Political Demands as well as Efficacy

harms of terrorism. They therefore fall into the areas marked "c" and "f." Either thoughtlessness put them into the "c" category or a desire to enjoy the benefits of a fictional new protection put them into the "f" category.

Finally, note that the choice of institutions to deal with the dangers presented by terrorism requires almost as much thought as the process of choice I have just described. Going back to Figure 8.1, we could assign the military, the FBI, Homeland Security, the CIA, or some other agency to deal through one of the ways generally reflected in one of the five rows with the goal of depriving the terrorists of one of the needs reflected in the nine columns.

When the steps that would be taken under one of the rows involves those in the United States, it may prove wise for the health of the institution and for the sense of security of the American public to avoid using either the military or a foreign intelligence agency. To look for the answer to what we should do—for example, what agency should gather intelligence at home—as part of a grand decision as to whether we are "at war" is to lose sight of the importance of an agency's culture and tradition in making an assignment that has risks to demo-cratic liberties.

Evaluating the Effectiveness of Our Responses to Terrorism, Even When We Know Very Little about Our Opponents

The process I have just described generates plausible alterna-tives, but it doesn't generate the critical analysis we need as to whether the alternative is flawed in the particular setting in which we hope to use it. I have said too little about evaluating the likely benefits of various alternatives. Any alternative is worth only as much as its chance of being effective in reducing terrorism. How can we assess that effectiveness?

Plans for handling terrorism can be wrong because they ignore or under-weigh other values such as domestic freedoms or foreign policy. That has been the focus of much of this book, along with reminders that steps which can reasonably be assumed to reduce terrorism in one plausible way may, and often will, tend to increase terrorism for another reason. But plans may also be wrong because they assume too readily erroneous factual connections between what we do and the level of terrorism. There is a partial remedy for the latter source of error. It is worth exploring carefully.

Every set of plans for dealing with an opponent or a number of opponents assumes certain causal connections between U.S. actions and the opponent's response (tactics) and also assumes broader causal connections between the overall plan and the overall set of responses that may seem possible and desirable to the opponent (strategy). For example, if the United States sets up a procedure to check more carefully the background of males 18–45 years old who are seeking to visit the United States from Arab countries, that tactic is based on a set of assumptions which includes:

• That future terrorists are likely to be male and young and from Arab countries;

• That at least a significant number of terrorists in this category will have backgrounds that can be matched with files at home or abroad; and

• That the review will prevent enough terrorists from coming into the United States to reduce the flow of terrorist events because the terrorists denied entry cannot be readily replaced.

Even if all the assumptions behind all the tactics are plausible or true, there are further assumptions behind the broader strategy. For example, we often assume that preventing conventional terrorist attacks will not disproportionately increase the risk of far more dangerous attacks with weapons of mass destruction or other mammoth explosions. Many students of the "war on drugs" believe that our success in preventing marijuana from coming into the United States from Colombia led directly to the substitution of the smaller and more easily hidden drug, cocaine, causing a far worse epidemic in the United States. The analogy is imperfect but at least cautions care in designing strategies.

One valuable check on our tactics and strategies in the fight against terrorism is first to identify the actions and plans on which we are relying and then, second, to list the most important assumptions on which our actions are based. The third step is to ask if there are alternative assumptions which are also plausible and which would throw into question a particular choice of actions. If there are—and there often will be—the prescription is not to do nothing in despair at our ignorance. We have to guess and act on our guesses. But we should simultaneously look for evidence that bears on the likelihood of one or another of the possible assumptions being correct. If the evidence starts to point in the direction of an alternative assumption that would undermine the reason for the actions we are taking, we have to either change our actions or develop still more evidence that either supports or challenges the actions on which we are depending for our safety.

For example, FBI Director Louis Freeh was severely criticized for not using polygraph (lie detector) tests periodically to review the reliability of agents with access to highly classified material, as the CIA already did. One such agent, Robert Hanssen, had been spying for the Soviet Union and then Russia over decades. There are, of course, value judgments critical to the decision whether to polygraph a certain class of employees, but there are also factual assumptions about the ratio of false positives to false negatives. A critical assumption behind recommendations to use the polygraph more systematically is that the harms caused by the frequency with which the test would fail to identify a spy (false negatives) or would cause needless disruption by falsely identifying as a spy an innocent employee (false positives) would be outweighed by the benefits of the times it correctly identified a "mole." A careful review of the factual assumptions by the National Academy of Science showed that, in this context, the number of false positives would be very great compared to the number of true positives and that there would be a failure to identify significant numbers of people who were, in fact, lying. Testing the factual assumptions is an important step in evaluating plans and in deciding whether to stick with particular tactics and strategies.

A wonderful example at the strategy level was presented by Professor Graham Allison in an op-ed article in the *Boston Globe*. The president's case for going to war with Iraq earlier rather than later relied on the argument that we might as well act promptly, despite grave risks that Saddam Hussein would respond by using biological or chemical weapons, because his capacities would only grow in the years ahead. The argument obviously assumed that Hussein's willingness to threaten weapons of mass destruction would not decline on its own and could not be reduced by us. But, Allison pointed out, this involved an additional assumption: that our ability to deal with biological or chemical attack would not increase more rapidly, in the following years, than Hussein's ability to harm us through such an attack. If that assumption was not true, then "later" was a better time than "sooner" to attack, if an attack proved necessary at all.

Consider how this form of evaluation can be used to assess our present tactics and strategies for dealing with Al Qaeda terrorism. A fair summary of our present plans to prevent terrorism (setting aside our plans for consequence management and retaliation) involves six steps:

• We will try to catch as many people associated with Al Qaeda as we can and incapacitate them;

• We will dismantle the organizational structure of Al Qaeda by attacking its leadership and denying it safe havens for recruitment, training, and planning;

• We will protect our most sensitive targets and attempt to deny Al Qaeda access to financial and other resources, including weapons of mass destruction. As one aspect of this, we will better patrol our borders, controlling who and what enters the United States;

• We will improve our own capacities for intelligence-gathering, combining information from a variety of sources, and predicting possible attacks so we can anticipate the plans of Al Qaeda in order to disrupt them before they can be carried out (as well as to identify and to incapacitate terrorists);

• We will use our economic, diplomatic, and military powers to get other nations to pursue those who might attack us when they are in other countries; and

• We will try to reduce support for Al Qaeda, and increase support for our attacks on terrorism, among: the populations abroad from whom it is recruiting and soliciting other forms of support; and the groups within the United States to which it might turn for tolerance or help.

Behind each of these steps there is a set of assumptions leading to the belief that the step will further the objective of reduced terrorism. We should carefully identify the most debatable assumptions on which particular plans or tactics rest. Take, for example, the so-far unsuccessful effort to disrupt the Al Qaeda organization by capturing enough of its leaders or by denying a secure place from which it can operate. If Al Qaeda is a top-down hierarchic organization with "sleeper cells" around the world in numbers that reflect the 10,000–15,000 people who went through Al Qaeda training camps in Afghanistan, the plan makes sense. By incarcerating the leadership of the Mafia in the United States, we substantially reduced the power of Italian organized crime and, at the same time, reduced its effectiveness and increased the ease with which we could thereafter monitor its activities. If Al Qaeda has a similar structure, the same strategy might work.

There are, however, alternate assumptions which are also possible and which, if true, would lead us to question our sharp focus on the Al Qaeda organization and its leaders:

• Al Qaeda may just be one embodiment of a very widespread Muslim or Arab anger at the United States which could and would be organized rapidly by successors if Al Qaeda were eliminated;

• Al Qaeda itself may not be a top-down hierarchy. It may be a loose network of Islamists deeply resentful of the United States, capable of identifying each other and willing to cooperate. There may be no leadership which activates and directs "sleeper cells." The cells may form and then dissolve with events in the Middle East or in the Muslim world and the relationship among them may be a network very different from a hierarchy; and

• The number willing to be "activated," even if our threat is largely from Al Qaeda and even if it is hierarchical in organization, may be very different from the number who attended training camps. The assumption that the training camps are like military training and therefore are ways of improving the skills of those who are already committed and who have already joined may be wrong. The training camps may be a recruiting device designed to bring those only partially committed to a place where some fraction can be encouraged to become terrorists by colleagueship and by Al Qaeda leadership. If so, the defeat of Al Qaeda in Afghanistan may substantially reduce the number potentially available to engage in terrorism.

In other words, there are alternative and plausible assumptions that would change our assessment of the importance and the effectiveness of one of the six categories of action on which we are basing an overall strategy. The alternative assumptions may be more or less plausible than those that underlie our plans. But their plausibility creates real risks; we are making a mistake to fail to take them seriously.

The way to give alternative assumptions the attention they deserve is to look for evidence that favors either our present assumptions or any plausible alternatives that would undermine the assumed effectiveness of our actions. The occurrence or discovery of any set of facts that would be more (or less) likely to be present depending on which assumption or hypothesis is true constitutes evidence changing our best guess as to the probability of each assumption. For example, it would be worth carefully examining whether the American-based groups that have been arrested for support of Al Qaeda first developed their plans and then took them to Al Qaeda, much like an academic might take a proposal for research to a foundation, or whether they went first to Al Qaeda and its training camps and only later developed their plans. The former would suggest a network organization or, at most, a single funding source. The latter would suggest a hierarchical organization. With a hierarchy, capture of those lowest down could, under the pressure of plea bargaining, lead to capture of a middle level. This could not happen if there was no hierarchy, although there may be other ways to exploit the trust required by a network (such as the use of undercover agents).

A Nation's Character

In sum, our national welfare, in the face of dangers of terrorism that may last for decades, depends upon our recognition that our pride in being Americans is as important to maintain as our skyscrapers, and that therefore political and moral stakes, and the courage of citizens, are as important as greater personal security. Thinking through choices wisely under pressure—that form of courage—is the critical skill.

That process begins with the realization that for security against terrorism we need, most of all, cooperative international intelligence and law enforcement activities, not bold attacks by a powerful military. We will also have to recognize that learning about the needs, motivations, and capacities of terrorist groups is essential, and that this process is not helped by thinking in terms of a war against pure evil. As we choose strategies we must see that extremely dangerous terrorism is likely to be around far longer than we can safely suspend democratic freedoms or our traditional separation of powers without losing the habits and attitudes democracy depends upon. The dangers from well-armed terrorists will, unfortunately, outlast any single embodiment, such as Al Qaeda and its associates. So must our democratic traditions.

In the end, even the new threats of terrorism measure our wisdom, courage, political responsibility, and dedication to what we proudly identify as American values more than they threaten our national security. Terrorist groups can attack and do damge but they cannot make war. They therefore almost never change regimes or even alter major policies. All terrorism can do is expose our deeper values and capacities as a democracy by stripping away the comfort of our feeling completely secure against foreign attacks. If underneath our feelings of security there lie courage and wisdom, terrorism will lose its capacity to generate a next generation of leaders. Only then will we be able to declare victory.

Notes

Chapter 1

1. Edward Cowan, "Quebec Extremists Escalate Separatist Campaign," *New York Times*, October 11, 1970, p. 174; Jay Walz, "Canada Invokes Wartime Powers in Quebec Terror," *New York Times*, October 17, 1970, p. 1; Edward Cowan, "Quebec Gets Note from Second Hostage, Renews Its Offer," *New York Times*, October 19, 1970, p. 1.

2. James Markham, "Terrorists Put Benign Belgium under Mental Siege," *New York Times*, February 6, 1986, p. A2.

3. The International Policy Institute for Counter-Terrorism, *Terrorist Organization Profiles: Red Army Faction (RAF)*, available at http://www.ict.org.il/inter_ter/orgdet.cfm?orgid=35; Flora Lewis, "The New Terrorism," *New York Times*, October 23, 1977, p. E1.

4. Office of the Coordinator for Counterterrorism, U.S. Department of State, Pub. No. 10687, *Patterns of Global Terrorism: 1999*, p. 78.

5. Ibid., pp. 19, 65.

6. These audiences include: the citizens of the nation attacked, or those whom the terrorists hope to recruit or have as supporters, or a minority part of the targeted population whom the majority is likely to alienate by its response.

7. For information regarding the relevant international law, see Matthew Lippman, "Genocide: The Trial of Adolf Eichmann and the Quest for Global Justice," *Buffalo Human Rights Law Review* 8 (2002), pp. 55, 106, 116; "Seizure and Trial of Eichmann Stir Widespread Legal Debate," *New York Times*, April 11, 1961, p. 14. For information on Adolf Eichmann, see Homer Bigart, "Trial of Eichmann Opens before Israeli Tribunal," *New York Times*, April 11, 1961, p. 1. For information on Enrique Camarena-Salazar, see Philip B. Heymann, *Terrorism and America: A Commonsense Strategy for a Democratic Society* (Cambridge, Mass.: MIT Press, 1998), pp. 50–51.

8. *Intelligence On-line* #448, March 6–19, 2003.

9. Elaine Sciolino, "Radicalism: Is the Devil in the Demographics?" *New York Times*, December 9, 2001, Sec. 4, p. 1; United Nations Development Program, *Arab Human Development Report 2002: Creating Opportunities for Future Generations* (New York: United Nations Publications, 2002), pp. 1–13.

10. Zahid Hussain, "How Al Qaeda Slipped Away," *Newsweek*, August 19, 2002, pp. 34–41.

11. At a press conference with President Jacques Chirac of France on November 6, 2001, President Bush announced that "You are either with us or against us." CNN, "You are either with us or against us" (November 6, 2001), available at http://www.cnn.com/2001/US/11/06/gen.attack.on.terror/. During his Address to a Joint Session of Congress and the American People, September 20, 2001, President Bush stated, "Either you are with us, or you are with the terrorists." Press Release, Office of the Press Secretary (White House), Address to a Joint Session of Congress and the American People (September 20, 2001), available at http://www.whitehouse.gov/news/release/2001/09/20010920-8.html.

12. Susan M. Akram and Kevin R. Johnson, "Race, Civil Rights, and Immigration Law After September 11, 2001: The Targeting of Arabs and Muslims," *New York University Annual Survey of American Law* 58 (2002), p. 295; Sameer M. Ashar, "Immigration Enforcement and Subordination: The Consequences of Racial Profiling After September 11," *Connecticut Law Review* 34 (Summer 2002), p. 1185; Adam Liptak, "After Sept. 11, a Legal Battle on the Limits of Civil Liberty," *New York Times*, August 4, 2002, Sec. 1, p. 1; Christopher Drew with Judith Miller, "Though Not Linked to Terrorism, Many Detainees Cannot Go Home," *New York Times*, February 18, 2002, p. A1.

13. The administration's proposed budget for 2003 requests $380 billion in defense spending, and $41 billion for domestic security. Elisabeth Bumiller, "Bush's $2.2 Trillion Budget Proposes Record Deficits," *New York Times*, February 4, 2003, p. A1.

Chapter 2

1. UN Charter, art. 2, sec. 4.

2. United Nations Treaty Series. "Geneva Convention Relative to the Treatment of Prisoners of War, August 12, 1949," art. 2, *Treaties and International Agreements Registered or Filed and Reported with the Secretariat of the United Nations*, 75, no. 972 (1950).

3. *Youngstown Sheet & Tube Co. v. Sawyer*, 343 U.S. 579 (1952).

4. *U.S. v. Hurst*, 6 C.M.R. 307 (A.B.R. 1952).

5. Johnny H. Killian and George A. Costello, eds., *The Constitution of the United States of America: Analysis and Interpretation. Annotations of Cases Decided by the Supreme Court of the United States to June 29, 1992* (Washington, D.C.: U.S. Government Printing Office, 1996), p. 309.

6. James Risen, "A Nation Challenged: The Threat; Qaeda Still Able to Strike the U.S., Head of C.I.A. Says," *New York Times*, February 7, 2002, p. A1.

7. Elaine Sciolino, "Don't Weaken Arafat, Saudi Warns Bush," *New York Times*, January 27, 2002, p. A1.

8. For discussion of the availability of weapons of mass destruction (WMD) and an outline for a plan on how to deal with terrorists' use of WMD, see Graham Allison and Andrei Kokoshin, "The New Containment: An Alliance against Nuclear Terrorism," *National Interest*, No. 69 (Fall 2002), pp. 35–43; Ashton B. Carter, Testimony before the Senate Committee on Armed Forces, *Arms Control & Nuclear Terrorism: A Global Coalition Against Catastrophic Terrorism*, August 1, 2002, available at http://www.senate.gov/~armed_services/statement/2002/August/Carter.pdf; Richard Lugar and Sam Nunn, "Connecting the Dots on Nuclear, Biological, and Chemical Terrorism: The Clear Danger and the Imperative of a Global Coalition Response," *Report on a Conference Sponsored by The Nuclear Threat Initiative (NTI), Moscow*, May 27, 2002, available at: http://lugar.senate.gov/052702a.html.

9. Allison and Kokoshin, "The New Containment."

10. See, for example, Herbert Krosney, *Deadly Business: Legal Deals and Outlaw Weapons: The Arming of Iran and Iraq, 1975 to the Present* (New York: Four Walls Eight Windows, 1993).

11. The Pew Research Center for People and the Press. "What the World Thinks in 2002: How Global Publics View: Their Lives, Their Countries, The World, America," released December 4, 2002 , at http://people-press.org/reports/display.php3?ReportID=165.

12. Ariel Merari, "Suicide Terrorism," Lecture, APA Convention, Chicago, August 2002.

13. Even talk of use of force by the United States looks like a crusade to some Muslims. See Safar Bin Abd Al-Rahman Al-Hawali, "Open Letter to President George W. Bush," available at http://www.muslimuzbekistan.com/eng/ennews/2001/10/ennews20102001.html.

14. "An I.R.A. Prisoner Dies in Belfast on the 61st Day of Hunger Strike," *New York Times*, July 8, 1981, p. A4; Dennis Kennedy, "Of Britain and Ireland," *New York Times*, May 20, 1981, p. A31; "Around the World; I.R.A. Prisoners in Ulster to Begin a Hunger Strike," *New York Times*, October 27, 1980, p. A7.

15. Bayan Rahman, "Japan Fails to Account for Plutonium," *Financial Times,* January 29, 2003.

16. Pierre Thomas, "Saudis Investigate Car as Getaway Vehicle; Freeh Presses for Greater Access in Bomb Probe," *Washington Post,* July 15, 1996, p. A13.

Chapter 3

1. Implicit in all the other steps, it must be able to carry them out in secrecy (or some of them with the secret tolerance of those who might otherwise prevent them) despite the intelligence efforts of both the United States and its allies.

2. UNDP, *Arab Human Development Report 2002,* pp. 1–13.

3. For information on Saudi schools, see Allan Gerson and Ron Motley, "Is Saudi Arabia Tough Enough on Terrorism," *New York Times,* December 30, 2002, p. A17; Thomas Friedman, "Dear Saudi Arabia," *New York Times,* December 12, 2001, p. A31; Thomas Friedman, "Drilling for Tolerance," *New York Times,* October 30, 2001, p. A17; Terrorism Q&A, The Council on Foreign Relations in Cooperation with the Markle Foundation, *Causes of 9-11: Arab Politics?* available at http://www.terrorismanswers.org/causes/arab.html. For information on Pakistani schools, see Jessica Stern, "Pakistan's Jihad Culture," *Foreign Affairs,* Vol. 79, No. 6 (November/December 2000), available at http://www.foreignaffairs.org/articles/stern1112.html.

4. Michael Barone, "By Silence Betrayed," *U.S. News & World Report,* October 22, 2001, p. 43.

5. Paul K. Davis and Brian Jenkins, *Deterrence and Influence in Counter-Terrorism: A Component in the War on al Qaeda* (Santa Monica: RAND, 2002), available at http://www.rand.org/publications/MR/MR1619/MR1619.pdf.

6. Caroline Kennedy-Pipe, *The Origins of the Present Troubles in Northern Ireland* (New York: Longman 1997), pp. 53–54.

7. Thomas Omestad, Larry Derfner, David Makovsky, and Khaled Abu Toameh, "Mideast: Any Way Out?" *U.S. News & World Report,* March 25, 2002, p. 12.

8. Merari, "Suicide Terrorism."

9. Roger Simon, Lisa Stein, Kim Clark, Mark Mazzetti, Mary Lord, Angie Cannon, Chitra Ragavan, Richard J. Newman, and Edward T. Pound, "Blown Away," *U.S. News & World Report,* September 14, 2001, p. 16.

10. Graham Allison, "We Must Act as if He Has the Bomb," *Washington Post,* November 18, 2001, p. B1; Allison and Kokoshin, "The New Containment."

11. Ashton B. Carter, Testimony before the Senate Committee on Armed Forces, *Arms Control & Nuclear Terrorism: A Global Coalition Against Cata-*

strophic Terrorism, August 1, 2002, available at http://www.senate.gov/
~armed_services/statemnt/2002/August/Carter.pdf; Ashton Carter and
Richard Lugar, "A New Era, a New Threat," *Financial Times,* Thursday, May
23, 2002, p. 15; Ashton B. Carter, "Throw the Net Worldwide," *Washington
Post,* Wednesday, June 12, 2002, p. A31.

12. In Tom Clancy's novel *Debt of Honor* (New York: Berkeley Books, 1995),
a Boeing 747 piloted by terrorists crashed into Congress during the president's
State of the Union Address.

13. Unpublished interview with Abu Abbas by Nasra Hassan (1998). [On file
with the author.]

14. Markle Foundation Task Force on National Security in the Information
Age, "Protecting America's Freedom in the Information Age" [hereinafter
Markle Foundation Report], p. 26, available at http://www.markle.org/
news/NSTF_Part_1.pdf.

Chapter 4

1. Neil J. Smelser and Faith Mitchell, eds., *Discouraging Terrorism: Some
Implications of 9/11* (Washington, D.C.: National Academies Press, 2002).

2. For a look at how these and other domestic and international issues
distracted the attention of the president and caused friction between the
administration and the FBI, see Elsa Walsh, "Louis Freeh's Last Case," *New
Yorker,* May 14, 2001.

3. *Brandenburg v. Ohio,* 395 U.S. 444, 447 (1969) ("[The] constitutional guarantees of free speech and free press do not permit a State to forbid or
proscribe advocacy of the use of force or of law violation except where such
advocacy is directed at inciting or producing imminent lawless action and
is likely to incite or produce such action."), *United States v. Rahman,* 189 F.3d
88, 119 (2d Cir. 1999) (words that "instruct, solicit, or persuade others to
commit crimes of violence ... violate the law and may properly be prosecuted regardless of whether they are uttered in private, or in a public
speech, or in administering the duties of a religious ministry").

4. *Scales v. United States,* 367 U.S. 203, 226 (1961) (when an organization
engages in criminal activity, "one who actively and knowingly works in the
ranks of that organization, intending to contribute to the success of those
specifically illegal activities" may be prosecuted).

5. For a brief look at how these German techniques have recently proven
useful in finding terrorists, see Douglas Frantz and Desmond Butler, "Imam
at German Mosque Preached Hate to 9/11 Pilots," *New York Times,* July 16,
2002, p. A3.

6. Robert O'Harrow, Jr., "Air Security Focusing on Flier Screening; Complex Profiling Network Months Behind Schedule," *Washington Post*, September 4, 2002, p. A01.

7. For a well-known example, see Samidh Chakrabarti and Aaron Strauss, "Carnival Booth: An Algorithm for Defeating the Computer-Assisted Passenger Screening System," *First Monday*, Vol. 7, No. 10 (October 2002); at http://www.firstmonday.org/issues/issue7_10/chakrabarti/index.html.

To maximize our success, we may need different levels of secrecy for different parts of our effort. While the actual sources of information might remain closely guarded, the methods used to analyze the information ("data mining") might be more widely discussed in order to involve the academic or business communities. The need for sophisticated data mining is not unique to the government. Businesses analyze customer records for buying habits and physicists analyze large collections of data from their experiments. The Defense Advanced Research Projects Agency (DARPA) has publicly provided information about its controversial "Total Information Awareness" system in order to solicit this public expertise. It has not, of course, revealed any of the specific sources of the information that the system might use.

8. Richard Willing, "U.S. Move Sparks Legal Questions," *USA Today*, June 11, 2002, p. 3A. The president's power to detain citizens captured in battle as illegal combatants was confirmed by the U.S. Court of Appeals for the Fourth Circuit in January 2003: *Hamdi v. Rumsfeld*, No. 02-7338, 2003 WL 60109 (4th Cir. 2003).

9. Robyn Blumner, "Did President Overstep in Detaining Suspects?" *Milwaukee Journal Sentinel*, July 22, 2002, p. 11A. However, two courts have asserted that these detentions are subject to judicial review. See *Hamdi*, 2003 WL 60109, at *6; *Padilla ex rel. Newman v. Bush*, No. 02CIV445 (MBM), 2002 WL 31718308 (S.D.N.Y. 2002).

10. The Foreign Intelligence Surveillance Act (FISA) permits the federal government to monitor people it believes to be foreign agents, but only if it has probable cause for that belief. See 50 U.S.C. §§ 1805, 1824. The government must submit proof to the Foreign Intelligence Surveillance Court (FISC)—a special, secret court created by FISA—in order to receive an order approving that surveillance. Many believe that, in practice, the necessary standard of proof is much lower than probable cause. From the inception of FISA in the 1970s until May 2002, when a rift between the FISC and the Department of Justice became public, FISC had disapproved just one government request for a surveillance order. See Dan Eggen and Susan Schmidt, "Secret Court Rebuffs Ashcroft; Justice Dept. Chided on Misinformation," *Washington Post*, August 23, 2002, p. A01. In addition, the Foreign Intelligence Surveillance Court of Review, which hears appeals from the government about surveillance orders that have been

denied, heard its first appeal *ever* in 2002. See *In re* Sealed Case, 310 F.3d 717, 719 (Foreign Int.Surv.Ct.Rev. 2002). Given the fact that applications for surveillance orders are almost never denied, it seems unlikely that a criminal standard of probable cause is required in every application.

11. Abu Abbas was arrested in Baghdad by American forces on April 15, 2003. James Risen and David Johnston, "'85 Hijacker Is Captured in Baghdad," *New York Times*, April 16, 2003, p. B1.

12. The use of assassination is still banned under executive orders. However, the Bush administration has authorized the killing of terrorist leaders, avoiding the limitations of the executive order by defining these terrorist leaders as enemy combatants. See James Risen and David Johnston, "Threats and Responses: Hunt for Al Qaeda; Bush Has Widened Authority of C.I.A. to Kill Terrorists," *New York Times*, December 15, 2002, sec. 1, p. 1.

13. Anthee Carassava, "Greece Reports First Breakthrough against Terrorist Group That Killed C.I.A. Agent in '75," *New York Times*, July 5, 2002, p. A6.

14. The self-defense standards set out by the Charter of the United Nations for when a state can use military force against another state do not deal with attacks by secret agents of another country (state-supported terrorism), nor do they specify what level of support for terrorist groups makes a state responsible as an aggressor and opens the possibility of self-defense. They do not specify what degree of certainty the responder must have and to whom, if anyone, it must demonstrate the evidence for its actions in self-defense. Nor do they specify whether secretly obtained evidence, such as by intelligence agencies, must be revealed in some measure, as President Reagan did before retaliating against Libya in 1985. The rules as to necessity and proportionality of response and as to permissible damage to civilian populations from bombing present major issues, as does the question of a state's responsibility for preventing war crimes by allied, sub-state forces.

15. Peter Finn, "Sept. 11 Plot Suspect Reportedly in Syria; German Citizen Being Interrogated," *Washington Post*, June 19, 2002, p. 3.

Chapter 5

1. News Release, American Bar Association, *American Bar Association Opposes Incommunicado Detention of Immigrants in Secret Locations* (August 13, 2002), available at http://www.abanet.org/media/aug02/immcomunicado.html.

2. David Margolick, "Israel's Payback Principle," *Vanity Fair*, January 2003, pp. 41–53.

3. For example, under the "Creppy memo," issued by chief immigration judge Michael J. Creppy on September 21, 2001, "[T]he Justice Department considers

all immigration hearings involving terror suspects off limits to the press and public, including the detainee's family." Charles Lane, "Court Calls for Open Detainee Hearings: U.S. Chastised on Immigration Case Secrecy Policy," *Washington Post*, August 27, 2002, p. A1; see also Adam Clymer, "Government Openness at Issue as Bush Holds onto Records," *New York Times*, January 3, 2003, p. A1.

4. Military Order, "Detention, Treatment, and Trial of Certain Non-Citizens in the War Against Terrorism," 66 FR 57833 (November 13, 2001).

5. See Neil A. Lewis, "Detention Upheld in Enemy Combatant Case," *New York Times*, January 9, 2003, p. A1.

6. Adam Liptak, "After Sept. 11, a Legal Battle over the Limits of Civil Liberty," *New York Times*, August 4, 2002, Sec. 1 p. 1.

7. See the report of the inspector general of the Department of Justice, "The September 11 Detainees: A Review of the Treatment of Aliens Held on Immigration Charges in Connection with the Investigation of the September 11 Attacks" (April 2003), at http://www.justice.gov/oig/special/0603/full.pdf, and Christopher Drew and Judith Miller, "Though Not Linked to Terrorism, Many Detainees Cannot Go Home," *New York Times*, February 18, 2002, p. A1.

8. Military Order, "Detention, Treatment, and Trial of Certain Non-Citizens in the War Against Terrorism," 66 FR 57833 (November 13, 2001).

9. Classified Information Procedures Act, 18 U.S.C. app. 3, §§1–16 (2000).

10. See Heymann, *Terrorism and America*, pp. 61–63.

11. Military Order, "Detention, Treatment, and Trial of Certain Non-Citizens in the War Against Terrorism," 66 FR 57833 (Nov. 13, 2001).

12. Philip Heymann, Testimony before the Senate Judiciary Committee, *Preserving Freedoms while Defending against Terrorism*, 107th Cong., 1st Sess., November 28, 2001, available at http://www.senate.gov/~judiciary/testimony.cfm?id=126&wit_id=68

13. Kennedy-Pipe, *Origins of the Present Troubles*, pp. 88, 114.

14. Greg Winter, "Some Mideast Immigrants, Shaken, Ponder Leaving U.S.," *New York Times*, November 23, 2001, p. B1; Jodi Wilgoren, "Swept Up in a Dragnet, Hundreds Sit in Custody and Ask, 'Why?'," *New York Times*, November 25, 2001, p. B5.

15. Fred Hiatt, "Democracy: Our Best Defense," *Washington Post*, November 19, 2001, p. A21.

16. Sam Dillon and Donald G. McNeil, Jr., "A Nation Challenged: The Legal Front; Spain Sets Hurdles for Extractions," *New York Times*, November 24, 2001, p. A1; William Safire, "Essay: Kangaroo Courts," *New York Times*,

November 26, 2001, p. A17; Marc Champion, John Carreyrou, and Gary Fields, "Europe Tour by Ashcroft Starts Sourly," *Wall Street Journal*, December 13, 2001, p. A18.

17. See Boris I. Bittker, "The World War II German Saboteurs Case and Writs of Certiorari before Judgment by the Court of Appeals: A Tale of None Pro Tone Jurisdiction," *Const. Commentary* 14 (1997), p. 451, citing Eugene Rachlis, *They Came to Kill: The Story of Eight Nazi Saboteurs in America* (New York: Random House, 1961), pp. 156–159. In 1942, eight Nazi saboteurs were arrested on U.S. soil and tried before a Military Commission. The FBI attributed the unmasking of the saboteurs to the extraordinary sleuthing of its agents although the proximate cause of their capture was the defection of one of the saboteurs.

18. Adam Liptak, "Traces of Terror: The Courts: Questions on U.S. Action in Bomb Case," *New York Times*, June 11, 2002, p. A18.

19. See, more broadly, Adrienne R. Bellino, "Changing Immigration for Arabs with Anti-Terrorism Legislation: September 11 Was Not the Catalyst," *Temple International and Comparative Law Journal* 16 (Spring 2002), p. 123.

20. Deborah Sontag, "Israel Court Bans Most Use of Force in Interrogations," *New York Times*, September 7, 1999, Sec. A, p. 1.

21. Israeli citizens, both Jewish and Arab, can be detained on security-related offenses for 15 days at most before being brought before a judge. "The Combined Initial and First Periodic Report of the State of Israel Concerning the International Covenant on Civil and Political Rights," U.N. Doc. CCPR/C/81/Add.13, 1998, para. 273–289. Further, in February 2003, the Israeli Supreme Court ruled that clauses of the Emergency Detention Order that enabled the military to hold Palestinian detainees between 12 and 18 days without judicial review were illegal. Press Release, the Association for Civil Rights in Israel, "Detaining Palestinians for 12 Days without Judicial Review Illegal" (February 27, 2003), at http://www.acri.org.il/english-acri/engine/story.asp?id=106. In terms of house demolitions, the owner of a house slated for demolition may appeal to the relevant military commander within 48 hours, and if that appeal is rejected, the home-owner has the right to appeal to the High Court of Justice. B'Tselem, "Demolition and Sealing of Houses as Punishment," at www.btselem.org. In the case of both administrative detentions and house demolitions, though, judicial review tends to be more formal than substantive, and in reality the courts rarely intervene. See, e.g., Press Release, B'Tselem, "IDF Holds 1007 Palestinians in Administrative Detention" (January 1, 2003), at www.btselem.org, and B'Tselem, "Demolition and Sealing of Houses as Punishment," at www.btselem .org.

22. *See Khaled A. F. Al Odah, et al. v. United States,* 2003 U.S. App. Lexis 4250 (D.C. Cir. 2003). This is not a radical departure from earlier U.S. case law regarding the treatment of aliens held outside the United States. See *Johnson, Sec. of Defense et al. v. Eisentrager,* 339 U.S. 763 (1950).

23. See *Yaser Esam Hamdi v. Donald Rumsfeld,* 316 F.3d 450 (4th Cir. 2003).

24. This position traditionally has been upheld by American courts. See *Ex Parte Quirin et al.,* 317 U.S. 1 (1942) (holding that the president could order that eight aliens accused of sabotage and espionage be tried before a military court).

25. In testimony before the Senate Judiciary Committee on December 6, 2001, Attorney General John Ashcroft stated "Congress's powers of oversight is not without limit [*sic*].... In some areas, however, I cannot and will not consult with you." For instance, according to Ashcroft, the president's authority to establish war crimes commissions arises out of his power as commander in chief, and so cannot be limited by Congress. "A Nation Challenged: Excerpts from Attorney General's Testimony before Senate Judiciary Committee," *New York Times,* December 7, 2001, p. B6; see also Neil Lewis, "A Nation Challenged: The Senate Hearing," *New York Times,* December 7, 2001, p. A1.

26. Adam Clymer, "Daschle Pushes to Query Security Chief," *New York Times,* March 15, 2002, p. A19.

27. Adam Clymer, "Government Openness at Issue as Bush Holds on to Records," *New York Times,* January 3, 2003, p. A1.

28. For the relevant court cases, see *Center for National Security Studies v. U.S. Dept. of Justice,* 215 F. Supp.2d 94 (D.D.C. 2002); Editorial, "A Win for Open Trials," *New York Times,* August 28, 2002, p. A18. The number of detainees is cited in Neil Lewis, "A Nation Challenged: The Senate Hearing," *New York Times,* December 7, 2001, p. A1.

29. *Detroit Free Press v. Ashcroft,* 303 F.3d 681 (6th Cir. 2002).

30. Frank Rich, "Slouching Towards 9/11," *New York Times,* August 31, 2002, p. A15. Seventeen Senators on the Senate Intelligence Committee were investigated in August 2002 concerning leaks about pre-September 11 NSA intercepts.

31. Avishai Margalit, "The Suicide Bombers," *New York Review of Books,* January 16, 2003, available at http://www.nybooks.com/articles/15979. This article asserts that groups using suicide bombers against enemy soldiers include Japanese kamikazis and Iranian basaji. Further, Chechens are now using suicide bombers against Russians; see Nick Paton Walsh, "Chechnya Suicide Bombers 'Used Russian Military Links,'" *The Observer,*

December 29, 2002, at http://www.observer.co.uk/international/story/ 0,6903,886123,00.html.

32. Martha Crenshaw, "The Effectiveness of Terrorism in the Algerian War," in Martha Crenshaw, ed., *Terrorism in Context* (University Park: Pennsylvania State University Press, 1995), pp. 473–513. See also, Bard E. O'Neill, *Insurgency & Terrorism: Inside Modern Revolutionary Warfare* (New York: Brassey's, 1990), p. 39.

33. Senate Select Committee on Intelligence, The FBI and CISPES, S. Rep. 101-46, at 102 (1989).

34. Office of the Attorney General, *Attorney General Guidelines on General Crimes, Racketeering Enterprise, and Domestic Security/Terrorism Investigations,* §III(B)(1), at http://www.usdoj.gov/ag/readingroom/generalcrimea.htm#domestic. The Guidelines state: "A domestic security/terrorism investigation may be initiated when the facts or circumstances reasonably indicate that two or more persons are engaged in an enterprise for the purpose of furthering political or social goals wholly or in part through activities that involve force or violence and a violation of the criminal laws of the United States."

35. Office of the Attorney General, *Attorney General Guidelines for FBI Foreign Intelligence Collection and Foreign Counterintelligence Investigations*, redacted copy on file with author.

36. *United States v. Verdugo-Urquidez*, 494 US 259 (1990).

37. Israeli Prevention of Terrorism Ordinance No. 33 of 5708-1948, Sec. 4(a)–(b).

38. Sec. 144B(A) of the Penal Law (Penal Law, 1986, 38 L.S.I. 230, [1986]).

39. *United States v. Rahman*, 189 F.3d 88 (2d Cir. 1999).

40. *Rice v. Paladin Enterprises, Inc.*, 128 F.3d 233 (4th Cir. 1997).

41. *Planned Parenthood of Columbia/Wilamette, Inc. v. American Coalition of Life Activists*, 290 F.3d 1058 (9th Cir. 2002).

42. Terrorism Act of 2000, §11, (1)—(2).

43. See Chapter 4, "Should the Ticking Bomb Terrorist Be Tortured?: A Case Study in How a Democracy Should Make Tragic Choices," in Alan Dershowitz, *Why Terrorism Works: Understanding the Threat, Responding to the Challenge* (New Haven, Conn.: Yale University Press, 2002), pp. 131–163.

44. In the twenty-five years since its creation in 1978, the Foreign Intelligence Surveillance Court has denied only one of the more than 10,000 wiretap applications it has received from the Justice Department. See Philip Shenon, "'Paper Court' Comes to Life over Secret Tribunal's Ruling on Post-9/11 Police Powers," *New York Times*, August 27, 2002, p. A12.

45. Assuming that each of the four predictions is independent of the others (as seems likely) and is 80 percent probable, the combined probability that all four would be true is 0.41.

46. Alistair Horne, *A Savage War of Peace: Algeria 1954–1962* (New York: Penguin, 1977), pp. 232–234.

Chapter 6

1. Charles Lane, "In Terror War, 2nd Track for Suspects; Those Designated 'Combatants' Lose Legal Protections," *Washington Post*, December 1, 2002, p. A01.

2. Such was the course of events in the Iran-Contra Affair. For a treatment of the subject authored by the independent counsel in charge of the Iran-Contra Investigation, see Lawrence E. Walsh, *Firewall: The Iran-Contra Conspiracy and Cover-up* (New York: W.W. Norton, 1997).

3. Thom Shanker and James Risen, "Rumsfeld Weighs New Covert Acts by Military Units," *New York Times*, August 12, 2002, p. A1. In November 2002, a pilot-less Predator aircraft launched a Hellfire anti-tank missile at a car in the Yemeni desert in which Qaed Salim Sinan al-Harethi (also known as Abu Ali), an Al Qaeda leader, and five companions were traveling. For more information, see James Risen and David Johnston: "Threats and Responses: Hunt for Al Qaeda: Bush Has Widened Authority of CIA to Kill Terrorists," *New York Times*, December 15, 2002.

4. William A. Orme, Jr., "Israel Cease-Fire Brings Some Calm, and Diplomatic Moves," *New York Times*, May 24, 2001, p. A6.

5. For a revealing account of the complexities of investigating terrorist acts such as the Khobar Towers bombing, see Elsa Walsh, "Louie Freeh's Last Case," *The New Yorker*, May 13, 2001.

6. The 12 international anti-terrorist agreements are: (i) the 1963 Convention on Offences and Certain Other Acts Committed on Board Aircraft; (ii) the 1970 Convention for the Suppression of Unlawful Seizure of Aircraft; (iii) the 1971 Convention for the Suppression of Unlawful Acts against the Safety of Civil Aviation; (iv) the 1973 Convention on the Prevention and Punishment of Offences against Internationally Protected Persons, Including Diplomats; (v) the 1979 Convention against the Taking of Hostages; (vi) the 1979 Convention on the Physical Protection of Nuclear Material; (vii) the 1988 Protocol for the Suppression of Unlawful Acts of Violence at Airports Serving International Civil Aviation; (viii) the 1988 Convention for the Suppression of Unlawful Acts against the Safety of Maritime Navigation; (ix) the 1988 Protocol for the Suppression of Unlawful Acts against the Safety of Fixed Platforms Located on the Continental Shelf; (x) the 1991

Convention on the Making of Explosives for the Purposes of Detection; (xi) the 1997 International Convention for the Suppression of Terrorist Bombings; and (xii) the 1999 International Convention for the Suppression of the Financing of Terrorism.

7. Bernard Lewis, "The Revolt of Islam: When Did the Conflict with the West Begin, and How Could It End?" *New Yorker*, November 19, 2001, p. 50; Husain Haqqani, "Islam's Medieval Outposts," *Foreign Policy*, November/December 2002, pp. 58–64. The Pew survey released in December of 2002 showed that 76 percent of Russians, 75 percent of French, 54 percent of Germans, and 44 percent of British believed that a desire to control Iraq's oil fields explained our policies there. See Pew Research Center for People and the Press, "What the World Thinks in 2002: How Global Publics View: Their Lives, Their Countries, The World, America," released December 4, 2002, at http://people-press.org/reports/display.php3?ReportID=165.

8. Peter J. Katzenstein: "September 11th in Comparative Perspective: The Anti-Terrorism Campaigns of Germany and Japan," unpublished paper, October 2001, available at http://www.einaudi.cornell.edu/9-11/content/pdf/pkatzenstein.pdf.

9. An illustration of the German sensibility can be seen in its investigation of suspected terrorist activities around Independence Day in 2002: see Charles M. Sennott, "In Europe, Concern for Rights Slows Terror War," *Boston Globe*, August 5, 2002.

10. Shanker and Risen, "Rumsfeld Weighs New Covert Acts by Military Units."

11. Douglas Jehl, "A Nation Challenged: Saudi Arabia; Holy War Lured Saudis as Rulers Looked Away," *New York Times*, December 27, 2001, p. A1.

12. The White House, *The National Security Strategy of the United States of America*, September 17, 2002, at http://www.whitehouse.gov/nsc/nssall.html.

13. Tim Weiner, "When the World Stood on Edge and Nobody Died Beautifully," *New York Times*, October 13, 2002, sec. 4, p. 7. A full copy of Guevara's words are available through the National Security Archive, Vladislav M. Zubok, "'Dismayed by the Actions of the Soviet Union': Mikoyan's Talks with Fidel Castro and the Cuban Leadership, November 1962," at http://www.gwu.edu/~nsarchiv/CWIHP/BULLETINS/b5a15.htm

Chapter 7

1. Elizabeth Becker, "Brookings Study Calls Homeland Security Plans too Ambitious," *New York Times*, July 14, 2002, p. 1; David Firestone, "Some

Conservatives Question the Value of Reorganizing Domestic Security," *New York Times*, July 1, 2002, p. A10.

2. From Executive Summary Redacted and Unclassified, DOJ-IG Report: FBI and Counterterrorism ... and FBI Response, A Review of the Federal Bureau of Investigation's Counterterrorism Program: Threat Assessment, Strategic Planning, and Resource Management, Report No. 02-38, September 2002.

3. Ibid.

4. Testimony of Director of the CIA, George Tenet, in "Excerpts from Testimony by CIA and FBI Leaders about Sept. 11," *New York Times*, October 18, 2002, p. A12. CIA Director Tenet also favored decentralization, at least of CIA functions. He referred to the 900 people now in the CIA's Counterterrorism Center and added: "So the whole focus is [to] build your infrastructure and get after this problem, and bring as many people to the fight as you possibly can around the world to augment your own numbers. And keep your eye focused on the target, and figure out what the right balance is between the people at headquarters and the people in the field, to get the tools out there where the operations are run, where the tracing needs to be done, the technical operations."

5. "Foreign Intelligence Collection Improvement Act of 2003," Bill to Establish the Homeland Intelligence Agency, and for other purposes. 108th Congress, 1st Session, February 13, 2003.

6. "The common denominator in these initiatives is that they concentrate all the powers normally accorded to security services into the hands of a single agency, in the name of battling what is now viewed as Western society's worst enemy. And it seems the likely consequences of such changes are being gradually accepted by government leaders on both sides of the Atlantic." From "Anti-Terrorism Fight Changes the Game," *Intelligence Online*, No. 444-9-22, January 2003, p. 1.

7. Christopher H. Pyle, "CONUS Intelligence: The Army Watches Civilian Politics," *Washington Monthly*, January 1970.

8. For information on COINTELPRO and the Church Committee Hearings, the Final Report of the Select Committee to Study Governmental Operations with Respect to Intelligence Activities of the United States Senate, 94th Congress, 2nd Session, 1976, can be found at http://www.icdc.com/~paulwolf/cointelpro/cointel.htm.

9. Johannes Andenaes, "General Prevention—Illusion or Reality?" in Sanford H. Kadish and Stephen J. Schulhofer, eds., *Criminal Law and Its Processes*, 7th Edition (New York: Aspen Law & Business, 2001), p. 122.

10. Army Appropriations Act, ch. 263, § 15, 20 Stat. 145, 152 (1878) (codified as amended at 18 U.S.C. § 1385 [1994]), cite from Matthew Hammond, "The

Posse Comitatus Act: A Principle in Need of Renewal," 75 *Washington University Law Quarterly* 953, note 1 (1997).

11. Sub-committee on Constitutional Rights, Senate Committee on the Judiciary, 93 Cong., 1st Session, *Report on Military Surveillance of Civilian Politics* [added italics], at p. 15, citing Joan Jensen, *The Price of Vigilance* (Chicago: Rand McNally, 1969), p. 124.

12. Ibid.

13. For example, the Privacy Act was passed in 1974, and in 1975, "In response to allegations and public concern regarding abuses of U.S. intelligence agencies, including the military, both the House and Senate established select committees to study the issue." Michele Ann Smith, "The United States Military and Domestic Intelligence: Lessons of the 1960s and 1970s," unpublished paper, 2002.

14. A case in point is the imprecise use of the term "assassination" in Executive Order 12,333. "The imprecise use of the word 'assassination' may have been intentional.... Thus, instead of being an absolute ban on assassination, the order reserves the right to mandate such an action solely to the President." Jami Melissa Jackson, "The Legality of Assassination of Independent Terrorist Leaders: An Examination of National and International Implications," *N.C.J. Int'l & Com. Reg.* 24 (Spring 1999), p. 671.

15. Foreign Intelligence Surveillance Act of 1978, Pub. L. No. 95-511, 92 Stat. 1783 (codified as amended at 50 U.S.C. §§ 1801–1811, 1821–1829, 1841–1846, 1861–62).

16. See David King and Kirsten Lundberg, "Congressional Oversight and Presidential Prerogative: The 1991 Intelligence Authorization Act," Kennedy School of Government Case Program, August 1, 2002.

Chapter 8

1. Dershowitz, *Why Terrorism Works.*

2. Military Order, "Detention, Treatment, and Trial of Certain Non-Citizens in the War Against Terrorism," §§ 2, 4, Federal Register 66, no. 222 (16 November 2001): 57,833.

3. *N. Jersey Media Group, Inc. v. Ashcroft*, 308 F.3d 198 (3d. Cir. 2002); Adam Liptak and Robert Hanley, "Threats and Responses: Legal Issues; Court Upholds Secret Hearings on Deportation," *New York Times*, October 9, 2002, p. A1.

4. For suggestions that the United States has sent terrorist suspects for foreign interrogation to countries where torture is routine, see "End, Means and Barbarity—Torture," *The Economist*, January 11, 2003, p. 1 (Special

Report); Dana Priest and Barton Gellman, "U.S. Decries Abuse but Defends Interrogations; 'Stress and Duress' Tactics Used on Terrorism Suspects Held in Secret Overseas Facilities," *Washington Post*, December 26, 2002.

5. Thom Shanker and James Risen, "Rumsfeld Weighs New Covert Acts by Military Units," *New York Times*, August 12, 2002, p. A1.

6. John Mintz, "On Detainees, U.S. Faces Legal Quandary; Most Experts Say Al Qaeda Members Aren't POWs but Taliban Fighters Might Be," *Washington Post*, January 27, 2002, p. A22.

7. *Silent enim leges inter arma*—"for the laws are silent among arms," Cicero, *Pro Milone*, 10.

8. For a discussion of the onset of the second intifada, see Alan Dowty and Michelle Gawerc, "The Intifada: Revealing the Chasm," *Middle East Review of International Affairs*, Vol 5., No. 3 (September 2001), pp. 38–53.

9. In 1971, Congress enacted 18 U.S.C. § 4001(a), which reads as follows: "No citizen shall be imprisoned or otherwise detained by the United States except pursuant to an Act of Congress."

Index

The Robert and Renée Belfer Center
for Science and International Affairs

Graham T. Allison, Director
John F. Kennedy School of Government
Harvard University
79 JFK Street, Cambridge MA 02138
Tel: (617) 495-1400; Fax: (617) 495-8963
http://www.ksg.harvard.edu/bcsia
bcsia_ksg@harvard.edu

The Belfer Center for Science and International Affairs (BCSIA) is the hub of research, teaching and training in international security affairs, environmental and resource issues, science and technology policy, human rights, and conflict studies at Harvard's John F. Kennedy School of Government. The Center's mission is to provide leadership in advancing policy-relevant knowledge about the most important challenges of international security and other critical issues where science, technology and international affairs intersect.

BCSIA's leadership begins with the recognition of science and technology as driving forces transforming international affairs. The Center integrates insights of social scientists, natural scientists, technologists, and practitioners with experience in government, diplomacy, the military, and business to address these challenges. The Center pursues its mission in four complementary research programs:

• The **International Security Program** (ISP) addresses the most pressing threats to U.S. national interests and international security.

• The **Environment and Natural Resources Program** (ENRP) is the locus of Harvard's interdisciplinary research on resource and environmental problems and policy responses.

• The **Science, Technology and Public Policy Program** (STPP) analyzes ways in which science and technology policy influence international security, resources, environment, and development, and such cross-cutting issues as technological innovation and information infrastructure.

• The **WPF Program on Intrastate Conflict, Conflict Prevention and Conflict Resolution** analyzes the causes of ethnic, religious, and other conflicts, and seeks to identify practical ways to prevent and limit such conflicts.

The heart of the Center is its resident research community of more than 140 scholars: Harvard faculty, analysts, practitioners, and each year a new, interdisciplinary group of research fellows. BCSIA sponsors frequent seminars, workshops and conferences, maintains a substantial specialized library, and publishes books, monographs, and discussion papers.

The Center's International Security Program, directed by Steven E. Miller, publishes the BCSIA Studies in International Security, and sponsors and edits the quarterly journal *International Security.*

The Center is supported by an endowment established with funds from Robert and Renée Belfer, the Ford Foundation and Harvard University, by foundation grants, by individual gifts, and by occasional government contracts.

Allison, Graham T., Owen R. Coté, Jr., Richard A. Falkenrath, and Steven E. Miller, *Avoiding Nuclear Anarchy: Containing the Threat of Loose Russian Nuclear Weapons and Fissile Material* (1996)

Allison, Graham T., and Kalypso Nicolaïdis, eds., *The Greek Paradox: Promise vs. Performance* (1996)

Arbatov, Alexei, Abram Chayes, Antonia Handler Chayes, and Lara Olson, eds., *Managing Conflict in the Former Soviet Union: Russian and American Perspectives* (1997)

Bennett, Andrew, *Condemned to Repetition? The Rise, Fall, and Reprise of Soviet-Russian Military Interventionism, 1973-1996* (1999)

Blackwill, Robert D., and Michael Stürmer, eds., *Allies Divided: Transatlantic Policies for the Greater Middle East* (1997)

Blackwill, Robert D., and Paul Dibb, eds., *America's Asian Allies* (2000)

Brom, Shlomo, and Yiftah Shapir, eds.,*The Middle East Military Balance 1999–2000* (1999)

Brom, Shlomo, and Yiftah Shapir, eds.,*The Middle East Military Balance 2001–2002* (2002)

Brown, Michael E., ed., *The International Dimensions of Internal Conflict* (1996)

Brown, Michael E., and Sumit Ganguly, eds., *Fighting Words: Language Policy and Ethnic Relations in Asia* (2003)

Brown, Michael E., and Sumit Ganguly, eds., *Government Policies and Ethnic Relations in Asia and the Pacific* (1997)

Carter, Ashton B., and John P. White, eds., *Keeping the Edge: Managing Defense for the Future* (2001)

de Nevers, Renée, *Comrades No More: The Seeds of Political Change in Eastern Europe* (2003)

Elman, Colin, and Miriam Fendius Elman, eds., *Bridges and Boundaries: Historians, Political Scientists, and the Study of International Relations* (2001)

Elman, Colin, and Miriam Fendius Elman, eds., *Progress in International Relations Theory: Appraising the Field* (2003)

Elman, Miriam Fendius, ed., *Paths to Peace: Is Democracy the Answer?* (1997)

Falkenrath, Richard A., *Shaping Europe's Military Order: The Origins and Consequences of the CFE Treaty* (1994)

Falkenrath, Richard A., Robert D. Newman, and Bradley A. Thayer, *America's Achilles' Heel: Nuclear, Biological, and Chemical Terrorism and Covert Attack* (1998)

Feaver, Peter D., and Richard H. Kohn, eds., *Soldiers and Civilians: The Civil-Military Gap and American National Security* (2001)

Feldman, Shai, *Nuclear Weapons and Arms Control in the Middle East* (1996)

Feldman, Shai, and Yiftah Shapir, eds.,*The Middle East Military Balance 2000–2001* (2001)

Forsberg, Randall, ed., *The Arms Production Dilemma: Contraction and Restraint in the World Combat Aircraft Industry* (1994)

Hagerty, Devin T., *The Consequences of Nuclear Proliferation: Lessons from South Asia* (1998)

Heymann, Philip B., *Terrorism and America: A Commonsense Strategy for a Democratic Society* (1998)

Heymann, Philip B., *Terrorism, Freedom, and Security: Winning without War* (2003)

Kokoshin, Andrei A., *Soviet Strategic Thought, 1917–91* (1998)

Lederberg, Joshua, ed., *Biological Weapons: Limiting the Threat* (1999)

Shaffer, Brenda, *Borders and Brethren: Iran and the Challenge of Azerbaijani Identity* (2002)

Shields, John M., and William C. Potter, eds., *Dismantling the Cold War: U.S. and NIS Perspectives on the Nunn-Lugar Cooperative Threat Reduction Program* (1997)

Tucker, Jonathan B., ed., *Toxic Terror: Assessing Terrorist Use of Chemical and Biological Weapons* (2000)

Utgoff, Victor A., ed., *The Coming Crisis: Nuclear Proliferation, U.S. Interests, and World Order* (2000)

Williams, Cindy, ed., *Holding the Line: U.S. Defense Alternatives for the Early 21st Century* (2001)